FUNatic's Guide to Walt Disney World 2012

Fun Facts and Hidden Mickeys

By Shannon and Ron Rasmussen

Dedication

We will never forget our first trips to Walt Disney World – experiencing the magic for the first time cannot ever really be replicated.

This book is dedicated to the incredible Wood Family, who shared our awe on our first few trips to Disney World.

Frank, Kristen, Natasha and Logan – We are so lucky to have been able to experience Disney World with your incredible family that very first time. The special bond your family experiences - which you extended to our family – will forever be a source of exceptional memories.

Doug, Stacy, Madison, and Jackson – We have never taken for granted how fortunate we are to be able to call your family a part of our extended family. Being able to visit Disney World with such an amazing family that is so full of positive energy has been a blessing for which we are grateful.

Jerry and Gaye – You remain an inspiration to us. That very first time we visited together, the rest of us were exhausted, and the two of you headed to Pleasure Island. To this day, your energy, positive outlook, and thirst for experiencing life to its fullest are motivating to us.

Introduction

Each year, millions of people flock to the magic of Disney World. Some of them go completely unprepared, "winging it" once they arrive. Others have planned in great detail the parks that will be visited each day, the meals the family will eat, and which attractions will be visited. Regardless of which type of park visitor your family is, the FUNatic's Guide to Walt Disney World – Fun Facts and Hidden Mickeys will enhance your visit. Or, if you don't have an upcoming trip, the book will give you the opportunity to learn some interesting information about this popular place.

The purpose of this book is to allow you to discover Disney in a very different manner. Guests become insiders, by learning all kinds of interesting and unusual facts about Walt Disney World. Plus, Hidden Mickeys are very popular at Disney World, and this book gives you directions to finding 84 different images of Mickey. As is true of the other FUNatic's Guides to Walt Disney World, you will also find many photos to enhance your exploration of Disney World.

This book was a natural addition to our complete set of FUNatic's Guides to Walt Disney World. The other books are designed to assist guests in their visits to Walt Disney World, or to relive the magic of previous trips. The project began as a single book, but after entering the huge amount of information about all of that Disney has to offer, the book became a four-book set: FUNatic's Guide to Walt Disney World: Magic Kingdom and Animal Kingdom, FUNatic's Guide to Walt Disney World: Epcot and Hollywood Studios, FUNatic's Guide to Walt Disney World: Resorts and Golf Courses, and FUNatic's Guide to Walt Disney World: Water Parks, Tours, and Downtown Disney. In addition to this book, there are also two other shorter, focused books, FUNatic's Guides to Walt Disney World: Eating and Drinking, and FUNatic's Guides to Walt Disney World: Rides and Attractions, that make it easy to carry to the parks for quick reference. The complete set has more information in one place than any other single source.

We want to thank the hundreds of guest photographers that have allowed us to include their photos in our books. Those photographs have only enhanced the information available to our readers.

Finally, our dearest hope is that this book allows you and your family to create a multitude of magical memories – much like the ones we continue to enjoy over time.

Navigating Through FUNatic's Guides

We have also created a way to know where to find each item in Walt Disney World. If you are looking at an item – let's say we are looking for the Hidden Mickey that is on the cover of this book – under the name of the item there will be a path listed which will visually show you where the item is located. In this case, you will see: Animal Kingdom => Camp Minnie-Mickey => Camp Minnie-Mickey Hidden Mickey which tells you that this Hidden Mickey is located within Camp Minnie-Mickey, which is located in Animal Kingdom.

You can also use the index in the back of the book to find particular items. The index is organized by location, so if you are in Magic Kingdom, you can go to the Magic Kingdom section of the index, and it will tell you where each Hidden Mickey can be located. You can also find out if there are any Fun Facts related to the park at which you are visiting.

Using Your FUNatic's Guide to Walt Disney World: Fun Facts and Hidden Mickeys

This unique book can really enhance a trip to Walt Disney World. You can simply read the various facts to learn some interesting things about this magical location. You can also use the guide strategically, by walking through the parks with your guide, reading about some of the places and items you come across as you undertake your trip.

You can also use the guide to create your own scavenger hunt. Take a picture of each Hidden Mickey, or see who in your group can find the most. Look for the various items that relate to the Fun Facts and memorialize the items in photos.

Even if you are sitting at home, reading the book cover-to-cover, you will find that your personal enjoyment of Walt Disney World is increased when you know these interesting "insider" pieces of information.

About Our Photographs

We use thousands of photos in our books. We have taken the majority of them on our various trips to Walt Disney World. Others are taken by fans of Walt Disney World who have been good enough to let us showcase their vacation photographs in our books for free. We value individual privacy rights, so unless we have a signed model release on file for every individual featured in a photograph, we blur or smudge the faces.

Send Us Your Photographs and Hidden Mickeys
Do you have a picture that you think really captures an element of Walt Disney World? Have you been able to get a great photo of a Hidden Mickey? Have you taken a photo that is missing from our book? If you would like one or more of your pictures to be considered for inclusion in the next publication of our book or on our Website, please visit www.FUNaticsGuide.com and click on "Submit My Pictures" for complete information. Also, please send descriptions of Hidden Mickeys that you think deserve inclusion in a future version of this book by emailing us: RonR@FUNaticsGuides.com.

Register Your Book
Register your book with us and get access to online coupons, join our discussion board, and receive notice of updates and new books. Visit www.FUNaticsGuide.com

Copyright

About the Authors

Probably the most complete Disney World book ever written, FUNatic's Guide to Walt Disney World was entirely a labor of love, combining the strengths of both Shannon and Ron. Shannon truly finds planning a trip to Disney World almost as much fun as the trip itself. Creating the trip plan allows her to completely immerse herself in Disney for months prior to a trip. Ron actually enjoys using technology to create ingenious ways to make life easier. When Ron used his computer skills to begin organizing the volumes of information that Shannon had been collecting during years of planning – and then undertaking – Disney trips, the idea for a book began taking shape.

The two of them have visited Disney World too many times to count during the past fifteen years. They have made it a goal to visit every park, resort, dining location, and entertainment opportunity as possible during that time. They have been there during the various holidays, special events, the most crowded times, as well as when the parks had fewer guests.

Shannon and Ron live in Washington State, and when they aren't in Disney World, Shannon is an 8th grade English teacher, and Ron owns a computer consulting company.

Table of Contents

Walt Disney World WDW

By: Darren Wittko

FUN Facts

🎇 There is a "formula" for how far apart the trash cans are in the parks: While eating a hot dog in Disneyland, Walt counted how many steps it took him to finish. Cans are spaced that many feet apart (17!)

This fun fact has multiple versions; the most common other story is that Walt handed out candy on opening day, and checked to see how far guests went before the wrapper ended up on the ground.

🎇 In Fantasia, the wizard's name is Yensid, which is Disney spelled backwards.

🎇 All castmembers that play Mickey must be between 4'6" and 5'2".

🎇 4% of ALL photos are taken at Disney World.

🎇 Disney World covers 40 square miles (about the size of San Francisco)

🎇 Of Disney World's more than 25,000 acres, less than 35% have been developed.

🎇 25% of Disney World is designated as a wilderness preserve.

🎇 Disney World has around 62,000 cast members.

🎇 Disney World is the largest single-site employer in the United States.

🎇 Mickey Mouse has more than 290 different costumes.

🎇 Minnie Mouse has over 200 costumes.

🎇 Cast members launder an average of 285,000 pounds of laundry every day.

🎇 Between 30,000 and 32,000 garments are dry-cleaned each day in Disney World.

🎇 More than 75 million Cokes are consumed each year in Disney World.

🎇 Disney World guests drink 13 million bottles of water each year.

- Disney World guests eat 10 million hamburgers each year.
- Disney World guests eat 6 million hot dogs each year.
- Disney World guests eat 9 million pounds of French fries each year.
- Disney World guests eat 300,000 pounds of popcorn each year.
- Every day an average of 210 pairs of sunglasses are turned into lost and found.
- Each year 6,000 cell phones are turned into lost and found.
- Each year 3,500 digital cameras are turned into lost and found.
- Each year 18,000 hats are turned into lost and found.
- Each year 7,500 autograph books are turned into lost and found.
- The most unusual items turned into lost and found are a glass eye and a prosthetic leg. Both items were claimed.
- More than 1.6 million turkey drumsticks are eaten every year in Disney World.
- It would take more than 68 years to stay in every guestroom in all of the hotels and resorts on Walt Disney World property.
- Nearly 12 percent of Walt Disney World property – an equivalent to nearly 3,000 football fields – is devoted to gardens and maintained landscapes.
- Each year a horticulture staff plants 3 million bedding plants and annuals on Disney World Resort property.
- Each year a horticulture staff maintain four million shrubs.
- Each year a horticulture staff maintain 13,000 roses.
- Both the Carrousel of Progress and "it's a small world" made their debut at the 1964-65 New York World's Fair.
- Vomit is called a protein spill in Disney World.
- Disney World sells more than 500,000 Mickey Mouse watches each year.
- Walter Elias Disney was born in Chicago on December 5th 1901.
- There are more than 350 chefs on staff at Walt Disney World Resort.
- More than 625 sommeliers have been awarded the Court of Master Sommelier Introductory Certificate at Disney World.
- Over 2.6 million chocolate-covered Mickey Mouse ice cream bars are sold every year at Walt Disney World Resort.
- More than a million pounds of watermelon are served every year at Walt Disney World Resort.
- There are over 200 designs of Mickey Mouse watches available at any given time.
- Walt Disney World's Costuming department has 2.5 million garment pieces.
- In 1964, as part of the "Florida Project," Walt Disney secretly started purchasing 27,433 acres of swampland in Central Florida for approximately $180 an acre.
- The entire length of the Disney World monorail system is 14.7 miles.
- Those giant turkey legs at Disney World have a whopping 1100 calories each.
- There are 470 places to eat a meal, a snack, or buy a refreshment in

Walt Disney World. This means a person can eat three times a day from March to August and never repeat a location.

❦ When purchasing land in Florida to build Walt Disney World, Walt used fake business names (like M. T. Lott and WEDway Enterprises) so that sellers would not know it was Walt Disney looking to buy the land.

❦ Seven Seas Lagoon is man-made.

❦ The "shoe tree" near Fort Wilderness in the Seven Seas Lagoon is decorated with the shoes of retiring Disney boat crewmembers.

❦ Newspapers can not be purchased inside the parks because they would ruin the illusion of fantasy.

❦ Each year, guests at Walt Disney World parks use 194,871 miles of toilet tissue.

❦ Every year, Walt Disney World guests eat more than 1.5 million soft pretzels.

❦ 8,000 tons of manure is the 4th largest recycled commodity of the Disney Company.

❦ Walt Disney World has been closed three times: the first time was after the 9/11 tragedy, and the subsequent closures were due to Hurricanes Frances and Charlie.

❦ It is hard to really conceive of the amount of laundry done at Disney World. It has been said that an individual could wash one load of laundry every day for 44 years, and that would be the same amount as the laundry done at Walt Disney World every single day!

By: Ron and Shannon   By; Ron and Shannon

FUNatics
Guide to
Walt Disney World
2012

Magic Kingdom

Magic Kingdom   Park

By: Ron and Shannon

FUN Facts

🎇 In Magic Kingdom, drinking fountains often come in pairs, one tall for adults, and one small for children. Some were actually designed so that when a parent and child are both drinking, they can look at each other!

🎇 As you walk from land to land in Magic Kingdom, be sure to look down - the ground changes to match the particular land.

🎇 The opening day crowd at Disney's Magic Kingdom Park was approximately 10,000 guests.

🎇 "E Ticket" Rides on opening day of Magic Kingdom were: Space Mountain, Pirates of the Caribbean, Haunted Mansion, Country Bear Jamboree, Hall of Presidents, Jungle Cruise, "it's a small world" and 20,000 Leagues Under the Sea.

🎇 The estimated annual attendance at Magic Kingdom is 17.2 million, followed by Epcot (10.9 mil), Disney's Hollywood Studios (9.7 mil) and Animal Kingdom (9.5 mil).

🎇 Magic Kingdom is the only theme park at Disney World that does not sell alcohol, and none of the parks sell cigarettes or gum.

🎇 The flag on the castle doubles as a transmitter for the Main Street Parades!

🎇 The small lumps of gum-looking substance on the ground in Magic Kingdom are actually float sensors.

🎇 It cost $400 M to build Magic Kingdom.

🎇 On average, fifteen children get lost each day in Magic Kingdom.

🎇 All of Disneyland would fit in the parking lot of Magic Kingdom.

🎇 When Disney's Magic Kingdom Park first opened its doors on October

1, 1971, adult admission cost $3.50.

By: Daryl Mitchell   By: Ron and Shannon

Jungle Cruise   Ride

Magic Kingdom=>Adventureland

By: osseous

FUN Facts

🌴 The friendly headhunter who appears near the end of the Jungle Cruise is known as "Trader Sam".

🌴 The Jungle Cruise water is dyed brown, so that guests can't see that it is only 3.5 feet deep in places!

🌴 Four rivers of the world are visited on the Jungle Cruise: the Nile, Amazon, Congo, and Mekong.

Hidden Mickeys

🐭 Sometimes waiting in line isn't so bad - you can find a great Hidden Mickey near the water of the Jungle Cruise, made-up of orange life preservers and black cleats.

🐭 A small Hidden Mickey can be found on the Jungle Cruise sign - look just under the J on the sign, and you will see three little bumps that form a classic three-circle Mickey head.

🐭 This one can be hard to find. Just after you pass the waterfall the first time, look for an airplane on the left side of the boat. On the right side of this wrecked plane, you can see a classic three-circle Mickey head kind of sketched into the aluminum body.

Pirates of the Caribbean   Ride

Magic Kingdom=>Adventureland

By: mrkathika

FUN Facts

☞ Check out the pirates playing chess in the queue of Pirates of the Caribbean - they are at a stalemate. They literally died playing chess... (Note: You must choose the right line of the queue to see the two pirates.)

☞ 125 Audio-Animatronics figures are used in the Pirates of the Caribbean - 65 are pirates and villages, and 60 are animals.

Hidden Mickeys

☺ As you are standing in line for one of the most popular rides in Magic Kingdom, be on the lookout for these Hidden Mickeys. If you find yourself in the left side of the queue, watch for the gun cases - many are locked with Mickey-shaped padlocks.

☺ As your boat approaches the final scene in Pirates, check out the green iron lantern that is hanging closest to the boat on the left side. There is a small three-circle classic Mickey formed by the wire loops hanging at the bottom of the lantern.

The Magic Carpets of Aladdin   Ride

Magic Kingdom=>Adventureland

By: osseous

FUN Facts

🐾 The Magic Carpets of Aladdin took flight in 2001, and is a 90 second excursion.

Hidden Mickeys

👀 There are many jewels embedded in the cement around the ride. Look for the jewels shaped like a Hidden Mickey about five feet inside of the queue. There are others in the area that also look like Hidden Mickeys, including a set near the shop.

By: Darren Wittko

By: tegioz

The Enchanted Tiki Room   Show
Magic Kingdom=>Adventureland

By: -Chupacabras-

FUN Facts
🌴 Originally known as the "Tropical Serenade," the Tiki Room in Adventureland was once sponsored by Florida Citrus Growers.
🌴 More than 300 Audio-Animatronics are included in the Enchanted Tiki Room, including flowers, statues and birds.

Hidden Mickeys
🐭 Hanging in each corner of the room are bird cages with a number of small birds in them. Look at the top part of the cage where the wire connects the cage to the ceiling. On one of the four cages - the one next to Pierre's perch - the connecting portion creates a three-circle Hidden Mickey.

By: Darren Wittko   By: Harshlight

Swiss Family Treehouse   Exhibit
Magic Kingdom=>Adventureland

By: Ron and Shannon

FUN Facts

🌿 The 60-foot-tall Swiss Family Treehouse in Adventureland weighs approximately 200 tons and is made of concrete and thousands of polyethylene leaves.

🌿 The tree holding the Swiss Family Treehouse is 90 feet in diameter.

🌿 There are 300,000 leaves on the Swiss Family Treehouse.

🌿 The original book, Swiss Family Robinson, was written in 1812. The Disney movie of the same name was produced in 1960.

Hidden Mickeys

🎃 Take a rest near the base of the Swiss Family Treehouse, on the stone benches with the wooden backs. While you are resting, check out the chunk of concrete between the two seat backs - sketched into the concrete is a whimsical Mickey head.

By: Chuck Kramer   By: Chuck Kramer

"it's a small world"

Magic Kingdom=>Fantasyland

Ride

By: Harshlight

FUN Facts

🌸 "it's a small world" in Walt Disney World holds 500,000 gallons of water.

🌸 "it's a small world" was created for the 1964 New York World's Fair.

🌸 Goodbye is written in 22 different languages at the exit of "it's a small world."

🌸 Originally, Imagineers wanted all the dolls in "it's a small world" to sing the national anthem from their own native country; however, you can imagine how difficult it might be to hear all the different songs. So, it was determined that one song, sang consistently throughout would be more cohesive.

🌸 In all of "it's a small world", there is only the name of one country actually inside the ride. You can find Mexico on a hat in the South America section of the excursion.

Hidden Mickeys

🐭 This Hidden Mickey is not at all obvious - until you know where it is! Take a look at the two towers where the ride operators sit. These are the ears of the Mickey. The head is formed by the captain's tower.

Dumbo The Flying Elephant   Ride
Magic Kingdom=>Fantasyland

By: Chuck Kramer

FUN Facts

🐘 Dumbo offers guests a 1.5 minute ride.

🐘 Dumbo was originally released in 1941. The film was re-released in theaters in 1949, 1959, 1972, and 1976

Hidden Mickeys

🐭 This Hidden Mickey is obvious, but not often seen. The fence surrounding the ride, along with two adjoining fenced garden areas create a giant Hidden Mickey!

By: Darren Wittko   By: d.k.peterson

Mad Tea Party   **Ride**

Magic Kingdom=>Fantasyland

By: mrkathika

FUN Facts

🌿 This ride is a tribute to Walt, as Alice in Wonderland was one of his favorite stories as a boy.

🌿 This attraction has different names in many of the five Disney parks. While it is Mad Tea Party in both Disney World and Disneyland, it is Alice's Tea Party in Toyko Disneyland, Mad Hatter Tea Cups at Hong Kong Disneyland, and Mad Hatter's Tea Cups in Disneyland Paris.

By: Gene Spesard

By: Harshlight

Peter Pan's Flight   Ride
Magic Kingdom=>Fantasyland

By: tegioz

FUN Facts
🏴 The blocks on the floor of the nursery in Peter Pan's Flight spell two different significant names: P Pan and Disney.

Hidden Mickeys
👂 This Hidden Mickey is very hard to find. Look carefully at the Peter Pan's Flight sign - at the spot where Peter Pan is standing in the clouds, it looks as if Peter Pan is standing on a Hidden Mickey.
👂 Look carefully at the ledge in the mermaid scene: three yellow flowers form a classic three-circle Mickey within the grass along the rocks.

By: Darren Wittko   By: d.k.peterson

Prince Charming's Regal Carrousel   Ride

Magic Kingdom=>Fantasyland

By: Ron and Shannon

FUN Facts

🌿 Built in 1917, Prince Charming's Regal Carrousel in Fantasyland was once located at Olympic Park in Maplewood, New Jersey.

🌿 You can find Cinderella's horse on Prince Charming's Regal Carrousel - it is the one with the gold ribbon on its tail.

🌿 There are 90 white horses on Prince Charming's Regal Carrousel; white is used because white horses signify "heroes".

By: mrkathika   By: tegioz

Snow White's Scary Adventures   Ride

Magic Kingdom=>Fantasyland

By: Ron and Shannon

FUN Facts

❦ The Wicked Queen appears regularly, overlooking Fantasyland, in an upper window just above Snow White's Scary Adventures.

Hidden Mickeys

🐭 Above the mirror in Snow White's Scary Adventures, when you see the old scary witch, you will find a classic three-circle Mickey head as part of the mirror frame.

🐭 Look at the laundry hanging on the line. One of the items is a set of boxers with Mickey's head on them.

By: Darren Wittko   By: Darren Wittko

The Many Adventures of Winnie the Pooh Ride

Magic Kingdom=>Fantasyland

By: mrkathika

FUN Facts

🏵 The Many Adventures of Winnie the Pooh at Fantasyland is located on the site of the former Mr. Toad's Wild Ride.

🏵 To commemorate Mr. Toad, whose ride was replaced by the Many Adventures of Winnie the Pooh, there is a photo in Mr. Owl's house within the ride of Mr. Toad handing the deed to the property to Owl.

By: Darren Wittko

By: Brian_Rechenmacher

Mickey's PhilharMagic 3D Spectacular   Show

Magic Kingdom=>Fantasyland

By: mrkathika

FUN Facts

🏴 The 150-foot wide and 28-foot high screen used in Mickey's Philharmagic is the largest seamless projection screen in the world.

Hidden Mickeys

👀 If you are a pro Hidden Mickey locator, this is one for you. It is harder to see due to the 3D nature of the film. Wait for the scene in which Ariel tosses jewels out in the sea. On the right side of the screen you will see a classic three-circle Mickey inside of the finger ring, while the ring is still rotating sideways.

By: Darren Wittko   By: tegioz

Cinderella Castle

Magic Kingdom=>Fantasyland

By: @cdharrison

FUN Facts

🌾 How many stones are there in Cinderella Castle in Magic Kingdom? NONE. The whole shell of the building is fiberglass.

🌾 Cinderella Castle is the third tallest attraction in Disney World (at 189 feet).

🌾 Some of the Mosaics at Cinderella's Castle have real gold in them.

🌾 The moat that partially surrounds Cinderella Castle contains 1.9 million gallons of water.

🌾 The coat of arms over the entrances of Cinderella's Castle are of the Disney family.

🌾 The Cinderella's Castle Suite contains three mosaics containing a total of 30,000 tiles made of Italian smalti glass. They feature a crystal slipper, a crystal pumpkin, the initials "WD" and a mouse looking up toward the castle.

🌾 During the winter holidays, 32,000 square feet of fish netting was used to help hang the LED lights on Cinderella's Castle.

🌾 As you look at Cinderella's Castle, you will notice that the bricks get smaller and smaller as you look higher on the castle. This is an example of "forced perspective" - the smaller bricks make the castle look taller.

Cinderella's Royal Table   Dining
Magic Kingdom=>Fantasyland

By: mrkathika

FUN Facts

❧ Prior to 1997, Cinderella's Royal Table was called King Stefan's Banquet Hall, named after Sleeping Beauty's father, King Stefan.

❧ The coats of arms on display inside Cinderella's Royal Table are a tribute to people who were significant in Walt Disney history. Some of the more than 40 coats of arms include: Roger Broggie, Sr., Roy Disney, Sr., John Hench, Diane Miller, Dick Nunis, Marc Davis, Marty Sklar, and Card Walker.

By: Harshlight   By: Harshlight

The Pinocchio Village Haus

Dining

Magic Kingdom=>Fantasyland

By: matt44053

FUN Facts

❦ If you sit inside of the dining area, you can watch the loading and unloading of the "it's a small world" boats.

❦ The main entrance to the utilidor tunnel is located underneath Pinocchio's Village Haus.

❦ The Cash Control area is located in the utilidor right beneath Pinocchio's Village Hause. Generally, vehicles powered with gasoline are not allowed in the tunnels due to vehicle fumes; however, Brink's armored cars, which are used for loading cash from the Cash Control area, are an exception of this rule.

By: Ron and Shannon

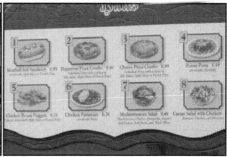

By: Ron and Shannon

Sir Mickey

Shopping

Magic Kingdom=>Fantasyland

By: Ron and Shannon

FUN Facts

🌱 If you look up at the roof of Sir Mickey's, you will discover the giant from Mickey and the Beanstalk peering in.

Hidden Mickeys

👀 Be sure to look closely at the Sir Mickey sign over the door - you will find a carved-out three circle Mickey.

By: Ron and Shannon

By: Ron and Shannon

Fantasyland Pin Kiosk

Magic Kingdom=>Fantasyland

Shopping Kiosk

By: Ron and Shannon

FUN Facts

❦ Guests are only able to purchase a maximum of two special edition pins per day.

Hidden Mickeys

🐭 Orange Mickey heads adorn the flag flaps of the small Fantasyland Pin Kiosk. You will also find classic Mickeys atop the flags on top of the kiosk.

Frontierland   Land

Magic Kingdom

By: Ron and Shannon

FUN Facts

🌱 In Frontierland, the addresses of the buildings refer to the year to which they are themed.

Hidden Mickeys

🐭 As you are strolling along the waterfront in Frontierland, near the Country Bear Jamboree, look over the rope fence - you will see a Hidden Mickey formed by a large barrel and two smaller bumper-like circles.

By: Dylan Ashe

By: Darren Wittko

Big Thunder Mountain Railroad Ride

Magic Kingdom=>Frontierland

By: hyku

FUN Facts

☞ Big Thunder Mountain Railroad in Frontierland features six trains: I.B. Hearty, I.M. Brave, I.M. Fearless, U.B. Bold, U.R. Daring and U.R. Courageous.

☞ Imagineers had to make the tunnels in Big Thunder Mountain Railroad taller, to allow people to raise their hands.

☞ Big Thunder Mountain Railroad is home to 20 Audio-Animatronics figures.

☞ Disney is known for their attention to detail - be sure to check out the crates in the queue of Big Thunder for a really amusing detail: one of the crates on the boxes says "Lytum & Hyde Explosives Company."

Hidden Mickeys

☞ While you are zipping along in the Wildest Ride in the Wilderness, look out to the right, just pass the dinosaur bones. You will see a classic three-circle Mickey created by a large set of rusty gears.

Splash Mountain   Ride
Magic Kingdom=>Frontierland

By: mrkathika

FUN Facts

🌿 Splash Mountain in Frontierland features a five-story, free-fall plunge at a 45-degree angle into a splash pool at a speed of 40 miles per hour.

🌿 Sixty-eight Audio-Animatronics are located throughout the Splash Mountain attraction.

🌿 It takes 20 minutes to fill, and five minutes to drain, the 965,000 gallons of water in Splash Mountain.

Hidden Mickeys

🐭 As you are floating along in your log in Splash Mountain, look for the picnic/fishing scene. The small red and white classic Mickey head sitting between the orange flower and the picnic basket!

🐭 As your log is heading up the second hill, look at the barrels on the right side of the boat. Towards the bottom right of the pile of logs, you can clearly see a classic three-circle Mickey head.

🐭 Just as you head outside for the first time, while floating in your log, look for the huge water tank with Muskrat Moonshine painted on it. Above the S in Muskrat is some spilled aqua paint. In the center of that spilled paint is a classic three-circle Mickey head.

🐭 Sometimes a long ride line can be relieved by the opportunity to experience some interesting details. You can find a classic three-circle Hidden Mickey while standing in the queue, on the left wall. It is just as you go into the first tunnel - look for the huge wooden yoke - painted on the yoke is a red Hidden Mickey.

Tom Sawyer Island
Playground
Magic Kingdom=>Frontierland

By: Ron and Shannon

FUN Facts

🐾 A swinging suspension bridge leads from Tom Sawyer Island to Fort Langhorne, which was named after Samuel Langhorne Clemens (better known as Mark Twain).

🐾 The wooden rafts that transport guests to Tom Sawyer Island are named after characters from the novel: Tom Sawyer, Injun Joe, and Becky Thatcher.

Hidden Mickeys

🐭 There are so many places to explore on Tom Sawyer Island. While you are experiencing all of the treasures of the Island, visit Fort Langhorn. The rifle roost on the right side has a Hidden Mickey on the handrail. The Mickey, formed by a knot in the wood, is near the top of the tower.

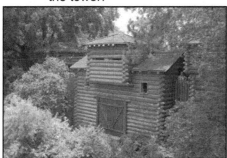

By: Chuck Kramer

By: Ron and Shannon

30

Country Bear Jamboree

Show

Magic Kingdom=>Frontierland

By: matt44053

FUN Facts

🌿 The three "talking heads" who introduce the Country Bear Jamboree are named Buff, Max and Melvin.

🌿 Eighteen bears perform in the Country Bear Jamboree, along with five other animals: a raccoon, a buffalo, a stag, a moose, and a skunk.

🌿 Look in the show waiting area for bear claw marks in the concrete on the floor.

By: Darren Wittko

By: Darren Wittko

Frontierland Shootin' Arcade   Arcade

Magic Kingdom=>Frontierland

By: mrkathika

FUN Facts

🔫 There are 97 different targets available in the Frontierland Shootin' Arcade.

Hidden Mickeys

🐭 While aiming for all of the great targets at the Frontierland Shootin' Arcade, keep your rifle trained on the cactus - from the right angle you can see that some of the parts of the cactus form a elongated Hidden Mickey.

Pecos Bill Tall Tale Inn & Café

Dining

Magic Kingdom=>Frontierland

By: Harshlight

FUN Facts

⚑ The Pecos Bill Tall Tale Inn was named in tribute of Pecos Bill, who stared in the Disney film, Melody Time in 1948. In the movie, Pecos Bill became famous for shooting all the stars in the Texas sky, making it the Lone Star State.

Hidden Mickeys

🐭 While you are standing in the checkout line at Pecos Bill, look up at the overhead lights. On the underside, you can see an etched Hidden Mickey.

By: Bradley_Jones

By: Ron and Shannon

Liberty Square

Land

Magic Kingdom

By: mrkathika

FUN Facts

🌿 The "Liberty Oak," in Liberty Square, is the proud parent of more than 500 young trees. They all started out as acorns harvested from the majestic oak.

🌿 All the flowers in Liberty Square are either red, white, or blue.

🌿 Because colonists removed the hinges from their shutters during the revolutionary war to make weaponry, the shutters on the buildings in Liberty Square in Magic Kingdom are all hanging slightly crooked.

🌿 The Liberty Tree contains thirteen lanterns among its branches, commemorating the thirteen original colonies.

🌿 There are no bathrooms located in Liberty Square, to honor the time period of this land.

🌿 There are so many details in Liberty Square that are easy to overlook. Check out the second story windows in this land. One has a rifle and another has two lanterns for "one if by land, two if by sea."

Haunted Mansion

Ride

Magic Kingdom=>Liberty Square

By: mrkathika

FUN Facts

☙ The Haunted Mansion uses state-of-the-art Omni mover vehicles called "Doom Buggies."

☙ The Haunted Mansion exit has crypts with names such as I.M. Ready, Rustin Peese, Pearl E. Gates, Manny Festation, Dustin T. Dust and Asher T. Ashes.

☙ In the Séance Room in the Haunted Mansion, Madame Leota (the disembodied head in the crystal ball) is actually a projection of the head of Imagineer Leota Toombs.

☙ The three hitchhiking ghosts names are Ezra (the tall ghost holding a hat), Phineas (the chubby ghost with a bag in his hand), and Gus (the short little convict ghost with the long white beard).

☙ When your "Doom Buggy" turns backwards, just at the caretaker, it indicates that you have joined the ghost world. In fact, you actually descend six feet, making you go "six feet under!"

☙ The Doom Buggies in the Haunted Mansion travel at about 1.4 mph and can accommodate up to 3200 guests per hour.

☙ The "stretching" rooms in the Haunted Mansions in Disneyland and Disney World move in different directions: at Disneyland the ceiling does not move; the floor goes down. However, in Disney World, the ceiling goes up and the floor stays in place.

☙ 109 animatronics are in the Haunted Mansion, 107 of which represent the ghosts living in the mansion. The other two are the mansion caretaker and his dog.

☙ The Haunted Mansion is the only attraction that is in a different land in each park's Magic Kingdom (Disneyland-New Orleans Square, WDW-Liberty Square, Tokyo-Fantasyland, Paris-Frontierland).

🎇 In the dining room scene of Disney's Haunted Mansion, the ghost is blowing out thirteen candles on the birthday cake.

🎇 Outside of the Haunted Mansion, you can find a carriage let by an invisible horse (known by many as Old Glue or Elmer). If you look at the ground, you will also see hoof prints in the concrete.

🎇 The black hearse that is outside of the Haunted Mansion was also used in The Sons of Katie Elder featuring John Wayne.

Hidden Mickeys

🐭 One of the most popular Hidden Mickeys can be found in the party scene of the Haunted Mansion. Look closely at the place settings on the table, and you will find one in the shape of a classic three-circle Hidden Mickey.

🐭 Look at the ancient maroon chair in the Haunted Mansion, near the vase filled with feathers, you will find a very rare Hidden Donald - look at the intricate design on the back of the chair.

🐭 At the end of the cemetery scene in the Haunted Mansion, on the front of the mausoleum near the Opera Singer, you can actually see the Grim Reaper holding a Mickey Head in his left hand. You have to look back to see this unique Hidden Mickey!

By: BoogaFrito   By: Chuck Kramer

Liberty Square Riverboat   Ride

Magic Kingdom=>Liberty Square

By: Ron and Shannon

FUN Facts

🏴 400 passengers can ride aboard Liberty Square Riverboat, which is 113 feet long, 26 feet wide, and 46 feet high.

🏴 The Liberty Square Riverboat is a steam boat that rides on a track around the Rivers of America.

Hidden Mickeys

👀 While not actually on the Riverboat, this Hidden Mickey is seen best from the deck. Look off the left side of the boat, toward Frontierland. There are several piers made up of rocks on the bridge to Splash and Big Thunder Mountains. There is a discernable three-circle Mickey among the rocks - one large rock for the head, with two smaller rock ears.

By: Darren Wittko

By: Harshlight

Hall of Presidents

Show

Magic Kingdom=>Liberty Square

By: str8jacket_atl

FUN Facts

- The Hall of Presidents originated as an Audio-Animatronic exhibition called "Great Moments with Mr. Lincoln," premiering at the 1964-65 New York World's Fair.
- In the second floor window of the Hall of Presidents there are two lanterns, referring to Paul Revere's famous line, "One if by land, two if by sea".
- Presidents Bill Clinton, George W. Bush, and Barack Obama are the only presidents to have actually recorded their own voices in the Hall of Presidents in Liberty Square in Magic Kingdom.
- 700 people can be seated in the Hall of Presidents.

By: Ron and Shannon

By: Ron and Shannon

38

Liberty Bell
Magic Kingdom=>Liberty Square

Point of Interest

By: QuesterMark

FUN Facts
- You can actually ring the Liberty Bell, but be prepared - the sound is impressively loud!
- The mold that created this replica of the Liberty Bell found in Liberty Square was cast from the original Liberty Bell located in Philadelphia. The same mold was used to create bells for every state in the US.

Stockade

Point of Interest

Magic Kingdom=>Liberty Square

By: Ron and Shannon

Hidden Mickeys

🐭 While not a perfect three-circle Mickey, check out the padlocks on the stockade - they are loosely the shape of a Mickey head.

Columbia Harbour House   Dining
Magic Kingdom=>Liberty Square

By: mrkathika

FUN Facts

🚩 To represent our country's change from British rule to self-governed, the Columbia Harbour House Restaurant has been decorated in a progressive style from Enlish to early American. As you enter the part of the restaurant closest to Peter Pan's Flight from Fantasyland(which, incidentally, was set in London), you will find English decorations. Then, as you walk through, the decor changes to colonial American.

🚩 Columbia Harbour House is one of only two locations in all of Liberty Square with an indoor bathroom (to honor the time period, in which there were no indoor bathrooms). The other indoor bathroom is located in another restaurant - The Liberty Tree Tavern.

By: Ron and Shannon

By: Ron and Shannon

Ye Olde Christmas Shoppe

Shopping

Magic Kingdom=>Liberty Square

By: mrkathika

FUN Facts

🖋 From the outside, the Christmas shop looks like three separate shops, but on the inside you will see that the walls are all open to make one large space. The story that goes with the buildings is that they were owned by three different colonial families--a German family, a woodcarver's family, and a musician's family.

🖋 Each day during the holiday season, a family is selected to decorate the shop's Magical Moments Christmas tree.

By: Ron and Shannon

By: Ron and Shannon

Main Street USA

Land

Magic Kingdom

By: Fugue

FUN Facts

🎺 Any Veteran may go to City Hall on Main Street and ask to participate in the daily flag ceremony at the end of the day!

🎺 The red sidewalks in Main Street were chosen to enhance the green of the grass.

🎺 The Dapper Dans - the barbershop quartet on Main Street - has a repertoire of over 100 songs that can be requested by guests.

Hidden Mickeys

👀 As you are wandering along, enjoying Main Street, be sure to soak in the many details. You can find a Hidden Mickey on the "Casting Agency" sign, between the Emporium and the Athletic Club. It is located near the top, as well as along the bottom, in the black border.

By: @cdharrison

By: @cdharrison

The Plaza Restaurant   Dining

Magic Kingdom=>Main Street USA

Hidden Mickeys

- While enjoying a delicious lunch in the Plaza Restaurant, take a look at the various pieces of wall art. If you find the one with the woman that looks like she is from the 1920s (she is wearing a hat that looks like flapper headwear, and is covered with small flowers), you might find a Hidden Mickey right above her head. The Mickey is a classic Mickey head, but the ears are both cut-off.
- Look carefully at the back side of the menu - while they aren't easy to find, if you scan carefully, you can find several Hidden Mickeys.
- Look for a Hidden Mickey at the entry of the Plaza Restaurant. You will find two bushes that have been trimmed into circles, that flank a larger brick circle; together, the three circles form the classic three-circle Mickey.

By: Ron and Shannon   By: Ron and Shannon

Tony's Town Square Restaurant   Dining

Magic Kingdom=>Main Street USA

By: Ron and Shannon

FUN Facts

🍃 Both Tony's Town Square Restaurant and Mama Melrose's Ristorante Italiano are based on Disney's Lady and the Tramp.

🍃 You can find two pair of dog paws, representing Lady and the Tramp, in the concrete in front of Tony's Town Square.

Hidden Mickeys

🐭 While indulging in wonderful Italian food, look for this "delicious" Hidden Mickey - it is located on the gorgeous marble-topped server beneath the Lady and The Tramp family photo. You will find a classic three-circle Mickey head molded out of bread inside a round basket.

By: @cdharrison

By: dawnzy58

Emporium

Magic Kingdom=>Main Street USA

By: mrkathika

Hidden Mickeys

🐭 A simple Hidden Mickey can be found on the metal legs that hold-up the shelves holding merchandise - little three-circle Mickey heads are punched out of the metal.

🐭 This Hidden Mickey can be somewhat hard to find. As you are looking up at the Emporium from Main Street, look for the stained glass windows. Each window has a circle that is flower-filled - that is the Mickey head. Above each flowered circle are two unsymmetrical ears that are bordered by green leaves.

Engine Co. 71 - Firehouse Gifts　　　Shopping
Magic Kingdom=>Main Street USA

By: Ron and Shannon

FUN Facts

🔥 A wall of real firehouse patches sent in by firemen from around the USA is located inside the Main Street Firehouse!

🔥 The Main Street Fire station, Engine Co.71, refers to the Magic Kingdom opening in 1971.

By: Ron and Shannon　　　　　By: Ron and Shannon

Main Street Confectionery

Shopping

Magic Kingdom=>Main Street USA

By: Chuck Kramer

FUN Facts

🐭 Look in the blue prints located in the window of the Confectionery - in one of the prints at the bottom of the window is an upside down Hidden Mickey.

Hidden Mickeys

🐭 While checking out everything available to satisfy a sweet tooth, be sure to notice the detail on the brass-colored candy containers. You will find small three-circle Mickeys right below the large round brass circle.

By: Ron and Shannon

By: Ron and Shannon

48

Tomorrowland   Land
Magic Kingdom

By: d.k.peterson

FUN Facts
🦜 There were two attractions open in Tomorrowland on opening day in 1971: Grand Prix Raceway and the Skyway to Fantasyland.

Hidden Mickeys
🐭 This Hidden Mickey is extremely difficult to find - as you are walking between Space Mountain and Buzz Lightyear's Astroblasters, you will find this very dim three-circle Mickey head carved into the cement under the Tomorrowland Transit Authority.

By: d.k.peterson   By: matt44053

Astro Orbiter

Ride

Magic Kingdom=>Tomorrowland

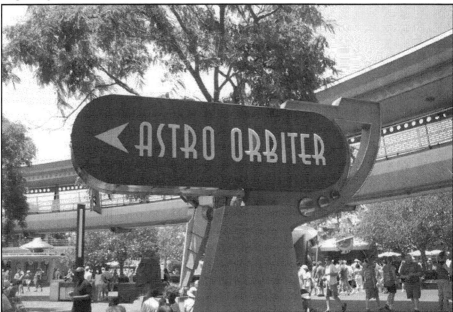

By: philosophygeek

FUN Facts

🕊 Astro Orbiter first opened in Tomorrowland in 1974 as Star Jets.

🕊 Revolving eleven times a minute, guests travel 3/4 of a mile during a typical ride on the Astro Orbiter.

By: Jaclyn Waldman

By: whiteshark29

Buzz Lightyear's Space Ranger Spin

Ride

Magic Kingdom=>Tomorrowland

By: Darren Wittko

FUN Facts

❦ Buzz Lightyear's Space Ranger Spin is located at the former site of If You Had Wings in Tomorrowland.

❦ Want to score big points in Buzz Lightyear? There are two high scoring targets - 100,000 points each - just as you are leaving the first room. You will have to turn your car all the way around, and shoot for the back of the orange robot's arm or the back of the buzz saw.

Hidden Mickeys

❦ As you are exiting Buzz Lightyear's Space Ranger Spin, after you have exited your car, you can see Stitch's spaceship outside the window in the mural on the right.

❦ Look for Mickey on a blue planet in the last target room - he is up in the top left corner on a map.

Space Mountain   Ride

Magic Kingdom=>Tomorrowland

By: Darren Wittko

FUN Facts

* Space Mountain is the fifth tallest attraction in Disney World (at 180 feet).
* Astronauts Scott Carpenter, Gordon Cooper and Jim Irwin were present at the grand opening of Space Mountain in 1975.
* 50,000 balloons were released to celebrate the opening of Space Mountain on January 15, 1975.

By: Darren Wittko

By: Darren Wittko

Stitch's Great Escape

Ride

Magic Kingdom=>Tomorrowland

By: mrkathika

FUN Facts

🏴 Stitch's Great Escape in Tomorrowland lies at the former site of ExtraTERRORestrial Alien Encounter, which closed in 2003.

🏴 To commemorate the opening of Stitch's Great Escape, Cinderella's Castle was "vandalized" by being wrapped in toilet tissue and graffiti.

🏴 In Stitch's Great Escape, Stitch is the first Audio-Animatronics figure to spit.

By: Darren Wittko

By: Darren Wittko

Tomorrowland Speedway   **Ride**

Magic Kingdom=>Tomorrowland

By: matt44053

FUN Facts

🏁 One of the original attractions at Disney's Magic Kingdom Park, Tomorrowland Indy Speedway, was once known as Grand Prix Raceway.

🏁 The Tomorrowland Indy Speedway goes 7.5 mph.

🏁 The cars at Tomorrowland Speedway cost $6,000 each, and have no brake pedal.

By: d.k.peterson   By: Ron and Shannon

Tomorrowland Transit Authority PeopleMover

Ride

Magic Kingdom=>Tomorrowland

By: mrkathika

FUN Facts

☞ The Tomorrowland Transit Authority was originally called the WEDway People Mover (WED standing for Walter Elias Disney).

☞ Each individual Tomorrowland Transit Authority PeopleMover tram follows its track 254 times, on average, in a typical weekend.

By: Darren Wittko

By: Darren Wittko

Monsters, Inc. Laugh Floor   **Show**

Magic Kingdom=>Tomorrowland

By: Ron and Shannon

FUN Facts

☞ Each show of the Monsters, Inc. Laugh Floor is different, since many of the jokes are texted by guests during the pre-show.

☞ The Visual Effects Society nominated Monsters, Inc. Laugh Floor for Outstanding Visual Effects in a Special Venue Project in 2008.

Hidden Mickeys

☺ Glance in the window display as you enter the attraction. You will see a domed building in the center of the city. Under the triangular roof top, you will see a classic three-circle Mickey head.

By: hyku   By: Darren Wittko

Walt Disney's Carrousel of Progress   Exhibit

Magic Kingdom=>Tomorrowland

By: meshmar2

FUN Facts

🌱 The audio-animatronic dog in the Carrousel of Progress is named "Rover".

🌱 In the 1940's scene, on the left wall of the daughter's room is a framed picture of Walt Disney.

🌱 Walt Disney's Carrousel of Progress debuted at the 1964 New York World's Fair. Then, it was moved to Disneyland in 1967. It was finally transported to Walt Disney World in 1975. Today you can see the revised version, completed in 1994.

Hidden Mickeys

🎭 Look for four Hidden Mickeys in the final scene: You will see Mickey as a nutcracker on the fireplace mantle, a stuffed Mickey as a gift, a white pepper mill on the kitchen counter, and an abstract painting in the dining room.

Cosmic Ray's Starlight Cafe   Dining

Magic Kingdom=>Tomorrowland

By: Ron and Shannon

FUN Facts

🌟 Cosmic Ray's is one of the largest indoor fast food restaurants in the world!!

🌟 Cosmic Ray's used to serve an "otherworldly" purple mayonaise and blue catsup.

🌟 Sonny Eclipse, an "intergalactic lounge singer," performs regularly at Cosmic Ray's Starlight Café in Tomorrowland.

By: mrkathika

By: Ron and Shannon

Merchant of Venus   Shopping
Magic Kingdom=>Tomorrowland

By: Ron and Shannon

Hidden Mickeys

🐭 In the mural behind the register, you can see a cute little soft tan alien holding a blue Mickey balloon.

🐭 Check out the mural behind the register in the shop - you will see a chubby purple alien wearing Mickey ears, standing up on the Tomorrowland Transit Authority platform.

By: Ron and Shannon   By: Ron and Shannon

Walt Disney World Railroad   Ride

Magic Kingdom

By: matt44053

FUN Facts

🎏 The Walt Disney World Railroad, which serves approximately 1.5-million passengers annually, is an authentic 1928 steam-powered train.

🎏 You will find a wooden leg labeled "Smith" in the Frontierland Train Station, commemorating the Mary Poppins tea party scene.

🎏 Walt built a train in his backyard called the Carolwood Pacific Railroad.

Hidden Mickeys

🎭 While standing at the base of the Main Street Walt Disney World Railroad station, check out the metal work at the top of the building. There are classic three-circle Mickeys, all along the scrollwork.

🎭 This Hidden Mickey is often missed by those that are hurrying through Disney World. Head upstairs of the Walt Disney World Railroad, and peek in the window of the small ticket office. Hanging on the wall is a gold-colored padlock, in the shape of a Mickey head.

60

Main Street Electrical Parade   Parade

Magic Kingdom

By: LaMenta3

FUN Facts

🌸 More than 80 performers appear in Disney's Main Street Electrical Parade.

🌸 The parade began in Disneyland in 1972. It did have a limited run in Walt Disney World from 1999-2001.

Mickey's Not-So-Scary Halloween Party

Fee-Based Activity

Magic Kingdom

By: Jeff_Kern

FUN Facts

🍃 During Mickey's Not-So-Scary Halloween Party, 216 tons of candy are given out to trick-or-treaters.

🍃 About 35 different varieties of candy are distributed to trick-or-treaters during Mickey's Not-So-Scary Halloween Party.

By: hyku

By: Ron and Shannon

FUNatics

Guide to

Walt Disney World
2012

Epcot

Epcot   Park

By: hyku

FUN Facts

🌿 10,000 construction workers were used to build Epcot.
🌿 There are 12,500 species of trees in Epcot.

By: wilsonken

By: Ron and Shannon

Chevrolet Design Center Ride

Epcot=>Future World=>Chevrolet Design Center Pavilion

By: mrkathika

FUN Facts

🏁 The crash test dummies in the queue area of Test Track are pounded in the chest, hit on the knee, and have their necks bent 720 times per day!

Hidden Mickeys

👂 As you are walking through the queue at Test Track, look for a red metal tool chest. Sitting among the mess near the tissue box and coffee mug, you will find a small plastic Mickey Mouse, peeking out of the pencil holder.

By: mrkathika   By: mrkathika

Journey Into Imagination with Figment   Ride

Epcot=>Future World=>Imagination! Pavilion

By: Chuck Kramer

FUN Facts

❦ 78 out of the 200 special effect patents created for the original Epcot center were used in Journey into Imagination with Figment.

Hidden Mickeys

❦ You get two-for-one in Journey Into Imagination with Figment - look for the large not-so-hidden pink cloud Figment in the wall. Then, just below Figment's mouth, you can find a tiny gold three-circle Mickey head in the orange hilly area.

By: Peter Dutton

By: Ron and Shannon

Captain EO

Show

Epcot=>Future World=>Imagination! Pavilion

By: Ron and Shannon

FUN Facts

🖋 In February, 2010 "Captain EO" replaced "Honey, I Shrunk the Audience", which originally took the place of "Captain EO" in 1994.

🖋 Captain EO cost about $1.76 million per minute to produce, for a total cost of around $30 million.

🖋 The two songs featured in the, "We are here to change the World" and "Another Part of Me" were both written by Michael Jackson.

🖋 EO in Greek means "dawn".

By: inazakira

By: inazakira

Mission Space Pavilion

Epcot=>Future World

By: mrkathika

FUN Facts

🦅 The wall that surrounds the pavilion says "Watch this SPACE". While the entire wall is covered with stars, there are several places where there are three stars placed close together to form the classic Mickey head.

Hidden Mickeys

🐭 The walkway leading to the Mission Space Pavilion, check the gem-bedecked concrete for several Hidden Mickeys. Several are pretty loose (the gem circles don't actually touch), but some are very clearly Hidden Mickeys.

Mission SPACE

Ride

Epcot=>Future World=>Mission Space Pavilion

By: mrkathika

FUN Facts

☞ The Mission: SPACE thrill ride at Epcot is so authentic that motion sickness bags are available just in case of emergency.

☞ It only takes six minutes to travel to Mars and back on Mission: SPACE.

☞ 100 shades of red were reviewed before Imagineers decided on the color of the red planet that is prominently featured in Mission: SPACE.

Hidden Mickeys

☺ In the Mission Space queue, peek into the control room. Periodically, you will see a class three-circle Mickey appear on the monitors that are overhead in the video.

By: Cory Doctorow   By: Ron and Shannon

Spaceship Earth   Ride

Epcot=>Future World=>Spaceship Earth Pavilion

By: Bradley_Jones

FUN Facts

🏴 Spaceship Earth's surface is made up of 11,324 aluminum and plastic triangles with gutters between them to allow for water drainage.

🏴 Spaceship Earth, the centerpiece of Epcot, weighs 16 million pounds – more than three times that of a space shuttle fully fueled and ready for launch.

🏴 Spaceship Earth is the forth tallest attraction in Disney World (at a whopping 183 feet).

🏴 Epcot's Spaceship Earth weighs 16 million pounds - equal in weight to 158 million golf balls.

🏴 The entire Spaceship Earth structure can fit inside of the Living Seas pavilion.

🏴 Four narrators have done the Spaceship Earth spiel in its history, starting with Vic Perrin. Walter Cronkite took Vic's place, followed by Jeremy Irons. When the attraction went through its last refurbishment in 2007, actress Judi Dench became the narrator.

🏴 To use Spaceship Earth as a golf ball, the golfer would have to be 1.2 miles tall.

The Land Pavilion

Pavilion

Epcot=>Future World

By: mrkathika

FUN Facts

🌿 More than 30 tons of fruits and vegetables grown at The Land pavilion at Epcot are served in Walt Disney World restaurants.

🌿 Five balloons hang in The Land pavilion. The middle one represents Earth, with the four surrounding balloons representing the seasons: Yellow for summer, Orange for Fall, Blue for Winter and Green for Spring.

🌿 The Land Pavilion is the largest in all of Future World. The pavilion is almost six acres.

By: mrkathika

By: mrkathika

Living with the Land   Ride

Epcot=>Future World=>The Land Pavilion

By: Darren Wittko

FUN Facts

🌱 Over thirty tons of food products, including fruit, vegetables, and seafood, are grown in The Land pavilion, and served at Walt Disney World restaurants.

Hidden Mickeys

🐭 While floating along in the Living with the Land attraction, be sure to look closely into the glassed room filled with test tubes - there is a classic three-circle Mickey in the center of the window.

By: Bob_Owen

By: Bob_Owen

Soarin' Ride

Epcot=>Future World=>The Land Pavilion

By: inazakira

FUN Facts

🕊 Guests board flight 5-5-0-5 for excursions on Soarin', which is a tribute to the date the ride opened (May 5, 2005).

🕊 Patrick, your flight attendant, is played by Patrick Warburton. He also played "Puddy" in Seinfeld, and currently plays "Jeff" on Rules of Engagement.

Hidden Mickeys

🐭 Get ready for it - while you are enjoying the pleasant ride on Soarin', watch for the golf scene. You will have to look quickly - the golf ball that is flying at you has a black Mickey head on it!

🐭 This Soarin' Hidden Mickey is hard to see, and even more difficult to capture in a photo. Check out the snow scene - right in the center, below the ridge off which the skiers jump - is a Hidden Mickey created out of black rocks nestled amidst the snow.

By: Cory Doctorow   By: hyku

# The Garden Grill   Dining
Epcot=>Future World=>The Land Pavilion

By: Ron and Shannon

FUN Facts

🚩 Be sure to check out the back pocket of Mickey's overalls; a fun detail is that the usual embroidered Wrangler W has been turned upside down to form an M, as a tribute to Mickey himself!

Hidden Mickeys

🐭 While eating in the top section of the restaurant, check out the various sunflower that are painted on the wall - many of them form Hidden Mickeys.

🐭 While standing near the railing as the restaurant rotates, look for the prairie dog scene. If you look carefully, you can see rocks placed in the shape of a Mickey.

🐭 This Hidden Mickey might require some help in locating, so ask a castmember at the Garden Grill. The mural with the fern has a very obscure, but satisfying, Hidden Mickey.

By: Ron and Shannon   By: Ron and Shannon

The Seas with Nemo & Friends

Ride

Epcot=>Future World=>The Seas with Nemo and Friends Pavilion

By: hyku

FUN Facts

- The artificial seawater in The Seas with Nemo & Friends pavilion has 27 truckloads of sodium chloride, better known as table salt.
- Renamed The Seas with Nemo & Friends in 2006, The Living Seas pavilion opened at Epcot in 1986 and was originally sponsored by United Technologies.
- Just one inch of water siphoned off the top of the Living Seas tank would fill a regular sized swimming pool (that's about 20,000 gallons.)

By: berkielynn

By: inazakira

Universe of Energy   Ride

Epcot=>Future World=>Universe of Energy Pavilion

By: Josh McConnell

FUN Facts

🌴 It took three artists 6,000 hours to paint the background diorama at the Universe of Energy.

🌴 At 45 minutes long (including the pre-show), Ellen's Energy Adventure at Epcot is the longest attraction in all of Walt Disney World.

🌴 In addition to starring in Ellen's Energy Adventure, Ellen Degeneres Is also the voice of Dory in Finding Nemo.

🌴 Ellen's final score is 17,300. (At least, that is her score before Final Jeopardy - they never show her score after she wins the contest.)

Hidden Mickeys

🐭 Watch for the man driving a tractor into a barn in the second half of the show. He drives a car out of the barn, and passes a church. If you look at the door of the church, you will see the shadow of the Earffel Tower!

Fountain of Nations

Point of Interest

Epcot=>Future World

By: Darren Wittko

FUN Facts

☛ The fountain at Epcot Innoventions Plaza can shoot water 150 feet in the air – within 30 feet of the top of Spaceship Earth.

☛ If all of the shooters of the Fountain of Nations in Epcot were fired at once, there would be 2,000 gallons of water in the air.

☛ 23 countries from around the world brought water from 23 different rivers and lakes to help feed the Fountain of Nations at its dedication ceremony.

Leave a Legacy

Epcot=>Future World

By: Ron and Shannon

FUN Facts

🏵 The huge granite sculptures range from 3 to 19 feet high. The heaviest one weighs more than 50,000 pounds.

🏵 The Leave a Legacy tribute walls were designed by Imagineer John Hench, who started his career as an artist with Disney in 1939. He also worked on the conception of Disneyland and was the chief designer of Spaceship Earth.

By: Ron and Shannon

By: Ron and Shannon

Where's the Fire?

Epcot=>Future World=>Innoventions West

Exhibit

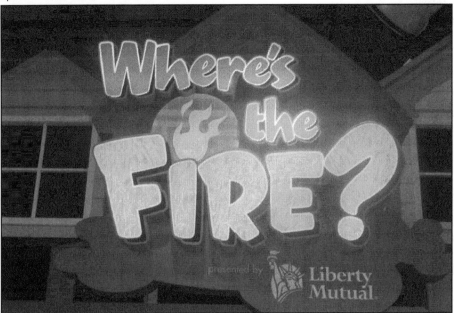

By: Ron and Shannon

FUN Facts

🔥 You can find a Hidden Goofy in Innoventions West, in the Where's the Fire display, on a magazine cover that hangs over a lamp on the back of the bed.

🔥 Where's the Fire is the largest fire prevention exhibit in the United States currently.

Hidden Mickeys

🐭 Take a peek at the bookends on the dresser in the Where's the Fire display in Innoventions West - they are Mickey heads!

By: Darren Wittko

By: d.k.peterson

Mouse Gear
Shopping

Epcot=>Future World

By: mrkathika

Hidden Mickeys

🐭 To find another great Hidden Mickey, spend some time in the huge Mouse Gear shop in Epcot: Look up on the wall, to the right of a huge painted Donald. You will find a classic three-circle Mickey assembled with three gold gauges.

🐭 While shopping for items in Mouse Gear, find the large metal structure with five circles cut out of it. The center circle has two large metal nuts that form the ears of the Hidden Mickey.

By: Ron and Shannon   By: Ron and Shannon

World Showcase

Epcot

Land

By: Darren Wittko

FUN Facts

🔥 More than 26,000 feet of lights outline the Epcot World Showcase pavilions – a string long enough to stretch across the Golden Gate Bridge more than six times.

🔥 The original plans for the World Showcase included 30 countries and an observation tower.

🔥 There are nineteen torches in World Showcase.

🔥 The entrance to the World Showcase is flanked by Canada and Mexico to symbolize the two countries that border the United States.

By: Ron and Shannon

By: Ron and Shannon

Canada

Epcot=>World Showcase

Country

By: dawnzy58

FUN Facts

🌿 The Hotel du Canada, the tallest of the structures in the Canadian pavilion, is three stories tall, but it is designed to look as if it is six stories.

Hidden Mickeys

🐭 As you are going into the Canadian pavilion, just past the steps, take a look at the left totem pole. You will find a black classic Mickeys on both sides near the top of the Raven's neck.

By: Harshlight

By: Harshlight

China

Epcot=>World Showcase

By: Harshlight

FUN Facts

🌾 Guests walk through the Temple of Heaven, which symbolizes the Chinese universe, to get to the CircleVision 360° theater.

Hidden Mickeys

🐭 Check out the banners in China - you might discover a three-circle Mickey head near the bottom of the banner.

By: Chuck Kramer

By: Ron and Shannon

France

Epcot=>World Showcase

By: mrkathika

FUN Facts

🚩 The Eiffel Tower in the French Pavilion is 1/10th the size of the original in Paris.

🚩 To keep birds from perching upon the Eiffel Tower in France, and thus ruining the illusion of size, the tower is coated with a sticky substance.

By: d.k.peterson

By: Harshlight

Germany

Epcot=>World Showcase

By: Darren Wittko

FUN Facts

🌂 The styles of the structures in the Germany pavilion represent different locations and periods in history. For example, the statue of St. George slaying the dragon in the town square represents the state of North Rhine-Westphalia and the Biergarten restaurant is Bavarian in style.

Hidden Mickeys

🐭 As you walk into the Germany pavilion, look at the building to the right (located just to the right of the Bier stand). You will see three kings on the building, above the doors - check out their crowns. The king in the center has a Hidden Mickey right in the middle of his crown.

By: Harshlight

By: QuesterMark

The Romantic Road

Exhibit

Epcot=>World Showcase=>Germany

By: Ron and Shannon

Hidden Mickeys

🐭 This Hidden Mickey is quite a challenge, because it moves often! Look for a small Mickey figurine posed somewhere within the village. Sometimes he is in a window, other times you will find him lurking in a doorway. He might even be out in the open, standing in the town square.

🐭 Hidden Mickeys along the Romantic Road change locations. Look for a Hidden Mickey that is cut into the grass somewhere in the display.

🐭 Sometimes the landscapers will stamp a Hidden Mickey in the dirt (usually in the farming areas) of the Romantic Road.

🐭 Another Romantic Road Hidden Mickey that varies sometimes can be found in the tiny bushes and shrubs, that are sometimes clipped to form a three-circle Mickey.

By: Ron and Shannon

By: Ron and Shannon

Biergarten

Epcot=>World Showcase=>Germany

By: Ron and Shannon

FUN Facts

🌾 26.2 miles of bratwurst are served every 60 days at the Biergarten restaurant in the Germany pavilion at Epcot. That, by the way, is the length of a marathon.

Hidden Mickeys

👀 As you are enjoying the German band onstage, check out the backdrop hanging behind them. Between the two mountains, there is a patch of snow on the ground that looks like an irregular three-circle Mickey.

By: Ron and Shannon   By: Ron and Shannon

Die Weihnachts Ecke

Shopping

Epcot=>World Showcase=>Germany

By: Ron and Shannon

FUN Facts

❦ It is German tradition that each year a pickle is hidden on the Christmas tree. The first child to find the pickle gets a special gift. The pickle tree in Die Weihnachts Ecke offers numerous opportunities to celebrate this German tradition.

❦ Die Weihnacts Ecke translates into "the Christmas corner" in German.

By: Ron and Shannon   By: Ron and Shannon

Italy

Epcot=>World Showcase

Country

By: mrkathika

FUN Facts

❦ Italy's 83-foot bell tower in the World Showcase is replica of the original Campanile in St. Mark's Square in Italy.

❦ Italy was planned to be much larger than it is now - originally, Disney had planned to add elements of southern Italy, like Roman ruins.

Hidden Mickeys

❦ As you enter the Italy pavilion from Germany, you will find a classic, but irregular, Mickey head formed out of leaves on the sculpture on the left corner.

By: Harshlight   By: Harshlight

Japan

Epcot=>World Showcase

Country

By: Harshlight

FUN Facts

🎏 The 83 foot tall Goju-no-to pagoda is the icon of the Japan pavilion, and was inspired by the seventh century Horyuji Shrine at Nara.

Hidden Mickeys

🐭 Japan hosts a Hidden Mickey in the pool with the large goldfish - look at the drain, and you will find a really clear three-circle Mickey.

By: Chuck Kramer

By: The_Consortium

Matsuriza

Epcot=>World Showcase=>Japan

By: The_Consortium

FUN Facts

❦ Taiko means "great drum" in Japanese. The drums date back centuries to celebrations and ceremonies in Japanese culture.

❦ The huge drums played by Matsuriza can be heard from the United Kingdom to Germany.

Mexico

Epcot=>World Showcase

By: d.k.peterson

FUN Facts

🌿 A control booth for Illuminations is on top of the Mexican pavilion.

🌿 The pyramid that tops the pavilion was inspired by third century Meso-American structures, existing prior to the Spanish colonization of central America; this particular pyramid is reminiscent of Chichén Itzá.

Hidden Mickeys

👹 As you are entering the pavilion, look at the concrete blocks - in the right corner, you will see a Mickey head in the hieroglyphic design.

By: Harshlight

By: Ron and Shannon

La Cava del Tequila

Lounge

Epcot=>World Showcase=>Mexico

By: Chuck Kramer

FUN Facts

- La Cava del Tequila serves 70 different kinds of tequila.
- Tequilas tastes range in price from $8 to $50.
- Tequilas tastes range in price from $8 to $50.

By: Ron and Shannon

By: Ron and Shannon

Morocco

Country

Epcot=>World Showcase

By: ElizabethTable4Five

FUN Facts

🌿 The Moroccan artisans purposefully created flaws in the pavilion because they believe that no one except Allah can create something that is perfect.

🌿 Morocco is the only pavilion that is hosted by the country's government.

Hidden Mickeys

👀 Visit the spot where Aladdin and Jasmine meet and greet in Morocco, and look at the mural on the wall behind where they stand - on the right side of the mural is a salmon-colored tower with a Mickey head window.

By: Eric Polk

By: Chuck Kramer

Souk Al Magreb

Epcot=>World Showcase=>Morocco

By:

Hidden Mickeys

🐭 Be sure to look for the Hidden Mickey, located on the door of the shop - three large golden platters form a traditional Mickey head. It is fun to note that the Hidden Mickey moves - it can be located anywhere on the doors leading into the shop, and maybe even on the outside wall of the building.

Norway

Epcot=>World Showcase

By: Scott Ellis

FUN Facts

🍃 On extremely busy days, the stand selling Carlsberg beer in Epcot's Norway pavilion empties a keg every 20 minutes!

Hidden Mickeys

🐭 Take a little trip inside the Stave Church, and find the Viking in the glass case. You will find a black three-circle Hidden Mickey woven in the decorative trim near the bottom of his salmon-colored tunic on his right leg.

By: Beau_B

By: Ron and Shannon

Maelstrom

Ride

Epcot=>World Showcase=>Norway

By: Ron and Shannon

FUN Facts

🏴 The longboats used on Maelstrom are inspired by the dragon-headed ships used by the Vikings.

🏴 The entrance to Maelstrom is in the Alesund style of architecture, which is often called Art Nouveau, meaning "new art". The style is often uses white stucco and stone-trimming.

Hidden Mickeys

🐭 One of the most charming Hidden Mickeys is above the ride loading area of Maelstrom - one of the Vikings in the huge wooden boat in the mural is wearing Mickey ears!

By: Darren Wittko

By: mrkathika

The American Adventure　　　　Country

Epcot=>World Showcase

By: mrkathika

FUN Facts

🦃 There are 44 flags on display in the American Adventure pavilion.

🦃 The American Adventure pavilion is a combination of several styles of buildings that would have been popular in colonial times - they represent buildings in Williamsburg, Philadelphia, and Boston. There is also a style reminiscent of Monticello, Thomas Jefferson's home.

🦃 If you look at the various clocks throughout the pavilion, many have the number 4 represented as IIII. In colonial America, they would use this representation of 4 instead ov IV as one might expect.

Hidden Mickeys

🐭 On the first floor, near the back of the rotunda, look for a large eagle, framed in gold. In the framing itself, you will find a series of circles with stars in them - at the corner of each frame is a classic three-circle Mickey.

By: inazakira

By: mrkathika

The American Adventure Show   Show

Epcot=>World Showcase=>The American Adventure

By: Richo.Fan

FUN Facts

🎇 American Adventure "Spirits of America" statues represent Adventure, Compassion, Discovery, Freedom, Heritage, Independence, Individualism, Innovation, Knowledge, Pioneering, Self-Reliance and Tomorrow.

🎇 Forced perspective, in reverse, is used for the building housing the American Adventure show. The five-story building was designed to look like it is two stories, since buildings were not that tall in colonial times.

🎇 The animatronic figures in the American Adventure were the first to actually talk; previously, the words spoken by animatronics were part of a soundtrack.

🎇 The animatronic figures in the American Adventure were the first to actually talk; previously, the words spoken by animatronics were part of a soundtrack.

Hidden Mickeys

🐭 The various murals on the walls of the American Adventure Show are a compelling art history of our country, but they also hide a Hidden Mickey. check out the painting that shows a wagon train - right above the front leg of the first oxen is a Hidden Mickey.

Spirit of America Fife & Drum Corps

Performance - Scheduled

Epcot=>World Showcase=>The American Adventure

By: Ron and Shannon

FUN Facts

🏵 The instruments used by the Spirit of America Fife & Drum Corps are reproductions of 18th-century instruments.

Hidden Mickeys

🐭 While listening to patriotic tunes, be sure to sneak a peak at the large drum - there is a classic three-circle Mickey head under the eagle insignia.

By: inazakira

By: Ron and Shannon

United Kingdom

Epcot=>World Showcase

By: mrkathika

FUN Facts

🖋 The reason the buildings in the UK are extended further on the upper levels is because these are replicas of the homes of wealthier folks. When they emptied their chamber pots and other garbage from the upper floors, since the building was extended, the rubbish would not land on the foot of their building.

🖋 The buildings throughout the United Kingdom are fashioned after different centuries: The Tea Caddy represents the 1500's, the building next to the Toy Soldier is supposed to be the 1600's, the plaster and wood buildings represent the 1700's, and the buildings of the 1800's tended to be stone.

🖋 It has also been rumored that another reason European buildings in the 1600's were built so that the upper level extended beyond the lower level was to save on taxes - the idea is that taxes were based on the square footage of the lower floor.

By: Ron and Shannon

By: Josh McConnell

Rose & Crown Pub and Dining Room

Dining

Epcot=>World Showcase=>United Kingdom

By: d.k.peterson

FUN Facts

- The Rose and Crown serves more Guinness than any single establishment in the WORLD!!
- The Rose & Crown Pub in Epcot has a specially designed ale warmer that can heat your Guinness to 55 degrees, the temperature favored by Brits.

By: Harshlight

By: sylvar

The Sportsman's Shoppe

Epcot=>World Showcase=>United Kingdom

By: Ron and Shannon

Hidden Mickeys

🐭 Be sure to look at the sign as you are entering the Sportsman's Shoppe. A fun Hidden Mickey is created with a tennis racket, football, and soccer ball.

By: Ron and Shannon

By: Ron and Shannon

Toy Soldier

Epcot=>World Showcase=>United Kingdom

By: mrkathika

FUN Facts

If you are visiting the Toy Soldier in the United Kingdom, head to the back of the shop in the character greeting area. On the lower cabinet shelf, near the old typewriter, you can find an envelope with Pooh's signature on it.

By: Ron and Shannon

By: Ron and Shannon

IllumiNations: Reflections of Earth

Show

Epcot=>World Showcase

By: Ron and Shannon

FUN Facts

🎆 $35,000 is spent on fireworks each night for IllumiNations: Reflections of Earth at Epcot.

🎆 There are around 1,000 computer-timed fireworks in the IllumiNations: Reflections of Earth show.

🎆 The Illuminations globe weighs 350,000 pounds (equivalent to 150 midsize cars.)

🎆 The themes of the Illuminations musical scores are, in order, Acceleration, Chaos, Space, Life, Adventure, Home, Celebration, and Meaning.

By: Harshlight

By: Ron and Shannon

Epcot International Flower & Garden Festival

Special Event

Epcot

By: BoogaFrito

FUN Facts

🌱 Around 500,000 plants are planted each year in the International Flower and Garden Festival.

🌱 The International Flower and Garden Festival features more than 1,000 butterflies.

🌱 Sixty different species of trees are planted for Epcot's International Flower & Garden Festival.

🌱 It takes a full year - over 24,000 cast member hours - to prepare for each Epcot International Flower & Garden Festival.

🌱 It takes 400 Walt Disney World horticulturists to install the Epcot International Flower & Garden Festival landscape, topiaries and exhibits.

Hidden Mickeys

🔘 Only at Epcot a couple of months every year in the spring, the International Flower & Garden Festival is host to many Hidden Mickeys. One of the largest, and most obvious, is in Future World on the shores of the lake. You can't miss the Hidden Mickey made up of flowers.

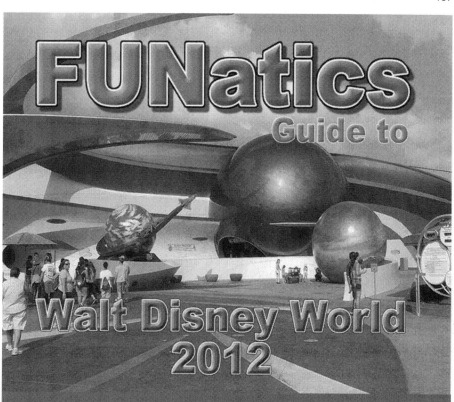

FUNatics
Guide to
Walt Disney World
2012

Hollywood
Studios

Disney's Hollywood Studios   Park

By: dawnzy58

FUN Facts

- The water tower in Disney's Hollywood Studios, the Earffel Tower, would wear a hat size of 342 ¾.
- Mickey would have to be 352 feet tall to fit in the sorcerer's hat that sits in the middle of Disney's Hollywood Studios.
- The Earffel Tower, the water tower which is one of Hollywood Studios' icons, is thirteen stories high, and has ears that weigh over two tons.

By: Darren Wittko

By: jdg32373

Voyage of the Little Mermaid

Show

Disney's Hollywood Studios=>Animation Courtyard

By: Ron and Shannon

FUN Facts

🎏 In the show, Ursula, the evil sea witch, is a huge puppet - she is twelve feet tall and ten feet wide.

Hidden Mickeys

🐭 Watch for Sebastian's entry in the show (he is tucked into a blue shell). Behind him, on his right, is a classic three-circle Mickey formed out of bubbles.

By: d.k.peterson

By: hyku

Honey, I Shrunk the Kids Movie Set Adventure   Playground

Disney's Hollywood Studios=>Backlot

By: Ron and Shannon

FUN Facts

🗡 The Honey, I Shrunk the Kids Movie Set Adventure park features a 52-foot long leaking water hose that sprays, 40-foot tall bumblebees, and 30-foot tall blades of grass.

Hidden Mickeys

🐭 This Hidden Mickey might be stretching it a bit. The railing next to the slide coming out of the roll of film has a very irregularly shaped three-circle Mickey.

By: Ron and Shannon

By: Ron and Shannon

Lights, Motors, Action! Stuntshow Extreme   Show

Disney's Hollywood Studios=>Backlot

By: hyku

FUN Facts

🍃 The Lights, Motors, Action! Extreme Stunt Show honors the 40 Walt Disney Imagineers and Cast Members who helped create the show with personalized license plates that contain the initials and birthdates of each designer.

By: Ill_Never_Grow_Up

By: The_Consortium

Muppet Vision 3D

Show

Disney's Hollywood Studios=>Backlot

By: Ron and Shannon

FUN Facts

🎺 Long Island University showed their respect for Kermit the Frog with an honorary doctorate degree in 1996.

🎺 As you approach Muppet Vision 3D, you will see a long brick wall on the right. With your eyes, follow the planters along the wall - the last one has an ice cream sundae in it, instead of flowers!

🎺 Want to find a Hidden Gonzo? Follow the pipe that is along the brick wall in the queue before you enter the waiting area - note the area where the pipe turns down in a 90 degree angle towards the ground. The pipe forms Gonzo's nose, and the rest of his face is drawn in in chalk.

By: Cory_Disbrow

By: mrkathika

Mama Melrose's Ristorante Italiano

Dining

Disney's Hollywood Studios=>Backlot

By: dawnzy58

FUN Facts

🖋 Mama Melrose's Ristorante Italiano at Disney-MGM Studios serves 720 pounds of pasta every day.

Hidden Mickeys

🐭 Look for the Hidden Mickey on the dalmation - it is one of his spots!

🐭 You can find a Hidden Mickey in the faux broken plaster on the left side of the archway.

By: hyku

By: Ron and Shannon

Toy Story Pizza Planet

Dining

Disney's Hollywood Studios=>Backlot

By: hyku

FUN Facts

🦅 The pizza parlor in the Toy Story movies, Pizza Planet, was originally going to be called Pizza Putt, which would have been a combination pizza parlor and mini-golf course.

🦅 The Pizza Planet truck that appears in all three Toy Story movies, has also appeared in every Pixar movie except the Incredibles.

Hidden Mickeys

🐭 Check the blue skies above this delightful quick service dining location for a small three-circle Mickey.

🐭 Look above the cash registers on the left, and you will find a classic three-circle Mickey in one of the constellations of stars.

By: Beau_B

By: mrkathika

50's Prime Time Cafe

Disney's Hollywood Studios=>Echo Lake

By: hyku

FUN Facts

🌿 At least 125 orders of meat loaf and mashed potatoes are requested every day at the 50's Prime Time Café.

🌿 Nestled in the space right next to the 50's Prime Time Cafe is the gated entrance for "apartments". The names on the mailboxes are tributes to numerous Disney Imagineers who were involved in the creation of Disney's Hollywood Studios.

🌿 The 1950's saw the advent of televisions in regular households, and with televisions, TV Dinners. 50's Prime Time Diner recognizes the popularity of the television, and serves comfort meals that were popular in those TV Dinners - like meatloaf, and fried chicken.

🌿 Guests of 50's Prime Time Cafe - both adults and children - might be chastised to "Take your elbows off the table," "Remove a hat," or "eat all your vegetables" by one of the joking servers. Oh, and if you use the restroom, be sure to wash your hands, and pay attention to the color of the soap - you may be asked upon your return to the table!

Tune-In Lounge

Lounge

Disney's Hollywood Studios=>Echo Lake=>50's Prime Time Cafe

By: Ron and Shannon

FUN Facts

❦ All of the televisions in the Tune-in Lounge, as well as in the 50's Prime Time Cafe, have the brand name, "Disney."

❦ Some of the television shows that play on the TVs in the Tune-in Lounge and 50's Prime Time Cafe are I Married Joan, Donna Reed, Make Room for Daddy, Dennis the Menace, the Mickey Mouse Club, and you can also see Walt Disney at Disneyland's opening!

Hidden Mickeys

☺ Be sure to scout around this charming lounge for a fun Hidden Mickey. The marbled Formica-topped coffee table has some interesting accents - black classic three-circled Mickey heads!

By: Ron and Shannon

By: Ron and Shannon

Min & Bill's Dockside Diner

Dining

Disney's Hollywood Studios=>Echo Lake

By: Ron and Shannon

FUN Facts

🏴 The name of the ship that houses the diner is "S.S. Down the Hatch."

🏴 The style of architecture of Min & Bill's Dockside Diner is known as California Crazy, and was popular in the 1930's. The idea of the style was to capture attention, and leave a long-lasting impression.

By: Ron and Shannon   By: Ron and Shannon

The Great Movie Ride

Ride

Disney's Hollywood Studios=>Hollywood Boulevard

By: mrkathika

FUN Facts

🏴 The Great Movie Ride at Disney's Hollywood Studios is housed in a replica of Mann's Chinese Theater.

🏴 There is only ONE ride in all of Walt Disney World (The Great Movie Ride) - all the rest are attractions. There used to be two rides, until the demise of Mr. Toad's Wild Ride.

Hidden Mickeys

👑 Find Mickey and Donald among the hieroglyphics in the first section of the Indiana Jones part of the Great Movie Ride. As you are leaving the throne room, look on the left side of the tram, just past a large silver statue. You will find it in the hieroglyphics, about eye-level, on about a 2-3 feet wide slab.

By: Darren Wittko

By: Chuck Kramer

The Hollywood Brown Derby

Disney's Hollywood Studios=>Hollywood Boulevard

Dining

By: osseous

FUN Facts

🖋 It is fun to examine the framed caricatures in the lobby area. The black-framed drawings are copies of the originals, while the gold-framed drawings are originals that came from the actual Brown Derby in Hollywood.

🖋 The Hollywood Brown Derby makes 31,000 Cobb salads every year.

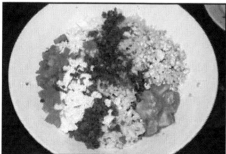

By: ElizabethTable4Five

By: osseous

Studios Backlot Tour   **Ride**

Disney's Hollywood Studios=>Mickey Avenue

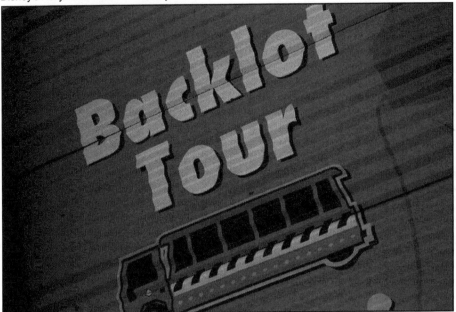

By: hyku

Hidden Mickeys

🐭 Check the blue sky during the Pearl Harbor scene of the Studios Backlot Tour - you will find a classic three-circle Mickey head among the clouds. Don't be fooled, though - while it is among the clouds, the actual Mickey is part of the bright blue sky.

🐭 This Hidden Mickey will only be seen by a very few people. In the first scene, the Pearl Harbor bombing, the guest that is chosen to be the mechanic during the demonstration can spy a Hidden Mickey on the left wall, underneath one of the knobs.

🐭 Shortly after taking off on the tram portion of the tour, you will see a cactus in the shape of a Mickey on the right side of the tram.

🐭 As you leave the Pearl Harbor show, and head towards the tram loading area, look for an aqua-colored refrigerator at the end of the first row in the prop area. There is a silver three-circle Mickey on it.

By: gordontarpley

By: gordontarpley

Streets of America

Street

Disney's Hollywood Studios

By: Daryl Mitchell

Hidden Mickeys

If you want to find a Hidden Mickey, wander along the Streets of America and enter the side street that has a locksmith sign on one of the buildings. Keep walking towards the end of the street, and find the area where people have signed their names in the concrete. In the curb is a chipped out Mickey Head – it is actually really easy to see.

This Hidden Mickey is quite nostalgic. Locate the building housing the "Venture Travel Service", and peek in the window. There is a framed picture of Walt himself, holding a Mickey Mouse doll.

Glimpse into Sal's Pawn Shop as you are walking along the Streets of America towards Lights, Motors, Action! Extreme Stunt Show. Hanging inside is a Mickey Mouse watch.

Osborne Family Spectacle of Dancing Lights

Point of Interest

Disney's Hollywood Studios=>Streets of America

By: Ron and Shannon

FUN Facts

☙ When viewing the Osborne Family Lights, hunt for a lit cat. Legend has it that one cat from the family's Halloween decorations got mixed with their Christmas lights when moving them to Disney World. The cat moves each year to a different location within the Osborne Family Spectacle of Dancing Lights, and it seems that he is more difficult to find each year.

☙ The original location for the Osborne Family Spectacle of Dancing Lights was on "Residential Street", where lights covered individual homes that were the sets of The Golden Girls, Matlock, Empty Nest, and others.

☙ Osborne Family Spectacle of Dancing Lights is made up of over 10 miles of rope lighting and connected by 30 miles of extension cords.

☙ It takes 20,000 man-hours to prepare the Osborne Family Spectacle of Dancing Lights each year.

Hidden Mickeys

☙ While there are many Hidden Mickeys within the lights throughout the Osborne Lights display, many move from year-to-year. This one can be consistently found in the steam coming out of the train display where you will find Santa Mickey engineering the train.

Stage 1 Company Store   Shopping
Disney's Hollywood Studios=>Streets of America

By: mrkathika

Hidden Mickeys
🐭 Want to find a Hidden Mickey that almost looks like a paint splatter? Go find the Kermit statue outside near the Stage 1 Company Store, and look for the spilled lilac paint - it ends in a little Hidden Mickey!

🐭 Look for the mural on the wall with the balloons - a classic three-circle Mickey head is formed by a pink balloon head, with blue and green balloon ears.

🐭 In the Stage 1 Company Store, located near the exit of Muppet Vision 3D, you will find several Hidden Mickeys. This one is located on a desk, which is often piled high with hats. Look for an aqua-colored paint stain that is in the shape of a classic three-circle Mickey (you might have to move some hats to see it!)

By: Ron and Shannon

By: Ron and Shannon

Rock 'n' Roller Coaster

Ride

Disney's Hollywood Studios=>Sunset Boulevard

By: berkielynn

FUN Facts

🎸 The Rock 'n' Roller Coaster – Starring Aerosmith at Disney's Hollywood Studios launches guests at a speed of 0 to 60 miles per hour in 2.8 seconds.

🎸 The track for Rock 'n Roller Coaster was built first, and then the building was created around it.

🎸 The doors in the queue of Rock 'n Roller Coaster are covered with 3,536 multicolored marbles.

Hidden Mickeys

🐭 A really fun Hidden Mickey exists in the queue, once you have gotten inside the building. Check out the carpet - in keeping with the 70's represented by the music in this attracting - a warped, psychedelic Mickey is clearly visible.

By: Harshlight

By: mrkathika

The Twilight Zone Tower of Terror **Ride**

Disney's Hollywood Studios=>Sunset Boulevard

By: Ron and Shannon

FUN Facts

🌴 The Twilight Zone Tower of Terror is the second tallest attraction in Disney World (just under 199 feet).

🌴 The Tower of Terror is mauve because it can be seen inside Epcot, behind Morocco; the color blends into the Moroccan pavilion.

Hidden Mickeys

🐭 Look for a Hidden Mickey in the preshow video, after you enter the library - the little girl is holding a Mickey doll.

🐭 Look at the dust-covered tables in the lobby of the Hollywood Tower Hotel while in the queue at the Twilight Zone Tower of Terror - you will find a Hidden Mickey made out of glasses. It is between a white hat and stack of books.

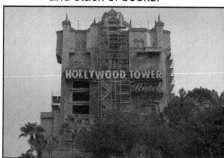

By: Harshlight

By: Harshlight

Fantasmic! Show

Disney's Hollywood Studios=>Sunset Boulevard

By: Harshlight

FUN Facts

☞ The pond surrounding the island is 1.9 million gallons of water but is only one-and-a-half feet deep.

☞ The 100-foot long and 16-foot high cobra that Mickey encounters in the show is the size of more than 8,000 average size king cobras.

☞ The water screens, upon which the various animated sequences are projected, are fifty feet high and 100 feet wide, which is over twice the size of an average theater movie screen.

By: Ron and Shannon

By: Ron and Shannon

FUNatics
Guide to
Walt Disney World
2012

Animal Kingdom

Animal Kingdom   Park

By: davef3138

FUN Facts

🌿 Animal Kingdom is five times the size of Magic Kingdom.

🌿 The baobab trees in Animal Kingdom are all man-made.

🌿 Disney's Animal Kingdom encompasses 403 acres.

🌿 Many of the benches in Animal Kingdom are made out of recycled milk jugs. (It takes 1,350 jugs to make one bench.)

🌿 $1.7 M per year is spent on worms to feed animals at Disney's Animal Kingdom.

🌿 It cost $800 M to build Animal Kingdom.

🌿 Sixty dump trucks full of dirt were delivered to the Disney Animal Kingdom construction site every day for two years to create the park's landscape.

🌿 Four million plants create the landscaping at Disney's Animal Kingdom.

🌿 Disney's Animal Kingdom is home to over 1,700 animals, representing 250 different species.

🌿 The animals at Disney's Animal Kingdom eat three tons of food each day (which is the amount the average person eats in 4 and a half years!)

Africa
Animal Kingdom

Land

By: Ron and Shannon

FUN Facts

Look up at the top of utility poles in Harambe, and you might see a Coke bottle used as an insulator for the power line.

Hidden Mickeys

Not actually a Hidden Mickey, but even more rare, you can find a Hidden Baloo in Africa in Animal Kingdom! He is part of the wall texturing, behind the Tamu Tamu refreshment stand, near the drums on the backside of the Tree of Life. This is often where Baloo & King Louie sometimes come out for their meet and greet. If you can't find the Baloo textured design, check behind the curtain.

Kilimanjaro Safaris

Ride

Animal Kingdom=>Africa

By: mrkathika

FUN Facts

🌿 The termite hills on the Kilimanjaro Safari are made out of concrete.

🌿 The entire Magic Kingdom could fit inside the Kilimanjaro Safari ride, with room left for parking.

Hidden Mickeys

😎 Considered the largest Hidden Mickey on Disney property, Flamingo Island itself, located in the Kilimanjaro Safaris, is shaped like a large three-circle Mickey head.

By: Chuck Kramer

By: Daryl Mitchell

Wildlife Express Train

Ride

Animal Kingdom=>Africa

By: mrkathika

FUN Facts

A round-trip excursion on the Wildlife Express train takes less than 15 minutes. Since the train holds up to 250 people, in a regular park day, there could be as many as 10,000 guests making the 1.2 mile excursion.

Hidden Mickeys

When you arrive at Rafiki's Planet Watch, be sure to look up at the roof as you pull into the station - you will see several Hidden Mickeys in the cross beams.

Tusker House Restaurant

Animal Kingdom=>Africa

By: Darren Wittko

FUN Facts

🌿 If you stand outside the Tusker House restaurant, you might hear the sound of banging dishes and discussions of employees - it is actually a recording!

🌿 The only live baobbb tree in Animal Kingdom is right outside of the Tusker House Restaurant.

🌿 The white "paint" on the outside of the baobab tree outside of the Tusker House contains nutrients and fungicides.

Hidden Mickeys

🐭 Look for the Assignment Board in the Tusker House, which hangs on the wall above a wood sideboard. There are a series of dots designating the jobs for various drivers - one of the dots has been made into a Hidden Mickey.

Mombasa Marketplace

Animal Kingdom=>Africa

By: Ron and Shannon

FUN Facts

The Mombasa Marketplace is named after East Africa's largest port city. Most people don't know that Mombasa is actually an island in Kenya.

Hidden Mickeys

If you keep your head down as you walk near the Mombasa Marketplace, you will discover a Hidden Mickey on the path that faces the Tusker House Restaurant. The face is formed from a utility cover with small rocks that form the ears.

Look high up in the Mombasa Marketplace, and you will see a series of nets. If you look closely, you can see three nets that overlap, creating a loose Hidden Mickey (this is disputed by some because the proportion is not quite right.)

Asia

Land

Animal Kingdom

By: Ron and Shannon

FUN Facts

🚩 In Anandapur, Asia's mythical land, there are actual prayer trees that are covered with flags and scarves intended to commemorate loved ones that have died and prayers. Bells are hung when the prayers are answered.

By: Chuck Kramer   By: Harshlight

Expedition Everest

Ride

Animal Kingdom=>Asia

By: Ron and Shannon

FUN Facts

❦ Expedition Everest is 199 feet tall because structures over 200 feet must have a lighted beacon atop them.

Hidden Mickeys

❦ Check out the teapot sitting on the table of various hiking gear items in the queue - it's bent form creates a Hidden Mickey!

❦ Be sure to check out the various exhibits in the queue of Expedition Everest - in one of the cupboards in Tashi's Trek and Tongba Shop, you will find a concrete yeti wearing black Mickey ears!

❦ The queue of Expedition Everest contains many interesting details - look in the cabinets along the back wall that are filled with food. In the corn cabinet, there are a series of yeti dolls - one of them is sporting Mickey Mouse ears!

Maharajah Jungle Trek   Self-Guided Walking Tour

Animal Kingdom=>Asia

By: Ron and Shannon

Hidden Mickeys

🐭 This Hidden Mickey is hard to find, but worth the effort! Find Mickey on a rock wall, with his green ears made out of leaves, just past the Tiger Exhibit in the deer exhibit - he is on the wall nearest to the tigers. Mickey looks a little like a space man, and, uniquely, he is waving at you.

By: Harshlight   By: Harshlight

Serka Zong Bazaar

Shopping

Animal Kingdom=>Asia

By: Ron and Shannon

FUN Facts

🦃 Look at the bottom of the display case with the orange paneling - there is a gold, peach, and green ribbon winding along the panel, and in the middle you can find a gold three circle Mickey head.

Hidden Mickeys

🐭 This Hidden Mickey is just across from the Serka Zong Bazaar: There are a series of concrete tablets on the left side. You will find a classic three-circle Hidden Mickey upside down on the second tablet from the edge, closest to the shop. As an identifying mark, the ears have a large ribbon (shaped like a smile) linking them.

By: Ron and Shannon

By: Ron and Shannon

Camp Minnie-Mickey

Land

Animal Kingdom

By: Bradley_Jones

FUN Facts

🌱 Peek over the bridge leading to Camp Minnie-Mickey, and you will see the Beastly Kingdom's Dragon's Lair. You can even see steam from his breath coming out of the dragon-shaped cave.

Hidden Mickeys

👀 As you are walking into Camp Minnie-Mickey, look into the trees to your right. You will see a birdhouse that has a very interesting opening - it looks just like Mickey Mouse!

By: mrkathika

By: Ron and Shannon

Festival of the Lion King   Show

Animal Kingdom=>Camp Minnie-Mickey

By: Ron and Shannon

Hidden Mickeys

☂ Look at the base of the Timon float (with the giraffe) - you will see a white classic three-circle Hidden Mickey within the purple triangles painted on the raised ridge.

By: Darren Wittko

By: Bradley_Jones

DinoLand U.S.A.   Land
Animal Kingdom

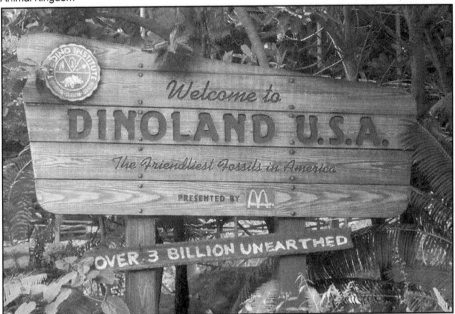

By: mrkathika

FUN Facts

Towering four stories over DinoLand U.S.A. at Disney's Animal Kingdom, Dino-Sue is an exact replica of the largest Tyrannosaurus Rex ever discovered.

Hidden Mickeys

After entering DinoLand U.S.A., find the dinosaur that is made out of concrete with many different rocks and ornaments stuck into the surface. Look for a silver broach, about the size of a quarter. Just above the broach, and below two small red stones, is a gold pin, with a Hidden Steamboat Willie embossed on it.

Primeval Whirl

Ride

Animal Kingdom=>DinoLand U.S.A.=>Chester & Hester's Dino-Rama

By: dawnzy58

Hidden Mickeys

🍭 Look at the 3D asteroid coming out of the sign - it is just under the brown dinosaur that is saying, "Head for the Hills." There is a three-circle Mickey hidden in the indents of the asteroid.

🍭 The asteroids seem to be popular places to look for Hidden Mickeys. Check out the main Primeval Whirl sign, and locate the 3D asteroid over the right side of the dinosaurs in the ride vehicle. You can find a three-circle Mickey created by the indents in the asteroid.

By: Jaclyn Waldman

By: Peter Dutton

DINOSAUR

Ride

Animal Kingdom=>DinoLand U.S.A.

By: Ron and Shannon

Hidden Mickeys

☙ This one is really hard to find. As your party exits DINOSAUR, look at the painted dinosaur mural behind the photo sales counter. Now, look under the farthest side of the dinosaur's mouth. The Hidden Mickey is located just between the glowing green-blue lines, just below the three gold raised bumps.

By: Chuck Kramer

By: mrkathika

The Boneyard Dig Site

Animal Kingdom=>DinoLand U.S.A.

Playground

By: mrkathika

FUN Facts

🌿 Children will want to explore the fossils on the wall. When they touch them, they will discover a surprise - the fossils are musical!

Hidden Mickeys

🐭 Peek inside the fenced storage area in the Boneyard - the fan and two hard hats for a fabulous Hidden Mickey!

By: The_Consortium

By: The_Consortium

Finding Nemo - The Musical

Show

Animal Kingdom=>DinoLand U.S.A.

By: Ron and Shannon

FUN Facts

🖋 Several songs in the show Finding Nemo - The Musical, were written by Tony-award winning musical composer, Robert Lopez, and his wife, Kristen Anderson-Lopez. The songs were inspired by actual lines from the movie, including, "Fish are friends, not food."

🖋 The Theater in the Wild, in which Finding Nemo - The Musical is presented, is the largest performance location in Animal Kingdom, holding up to 1,500 guests.

By: dawnzy58

By: mjuzenas

Dino-Sue

Animal Kingdom=>DinoLand U.S.A.

By: Loren R. Javier

FUN Facts

🌿 The real Dino-Sue, a Tyrannosaurus Rex, was 28 years old when she died (which made her the oldest T-Rex known.)

🌿 A Tyrannosaurus Rex had approximately 200 bones - around the same number as a human!

Cretacious Trail
Animal Kingdom=>DinoLand U.S.A.

Self-Guided Walking Tour

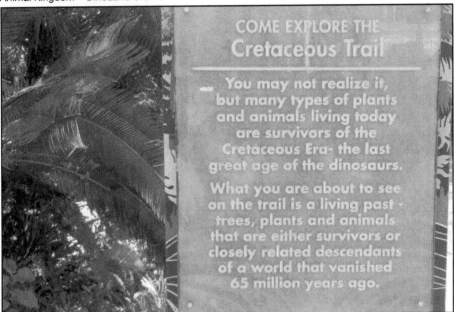

By: Ron and Shannon

FUN Facts
🌿 The Cretaceous Trail contains a set of cycads (a seedy plant) that is the third largest collection in Norh America. Furthermore, some of them are descendants of plants that date back hundreds of millions of years.

Hidden Mickeys
🐭 Look for the black three-circle Hidden Mickey on the back of the large dinosaur on which children often climb.

By: Ron and Shannon   By: Ron and Shannon

It's Tough to be a Bug! Show

Animal Kingdom=>Discovery Island

By: Ron and Shannon

FUN Facts

🐛 The 3-D glasses in It's Tough to be a Bug! are called "bug-eyes".

🐛 The It's Tough to be a Bug! theater holds up to 430 people, and empties every 15 minutes for a new show. That means, conceivably, there could be up to 17,200 people viewing this show in a single day.

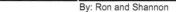

By: hyku   By: Ron and Shannon

Tree of Life
Animal Kingdom=>Discovery Island

Point of Interest

By: hyku

FUN Facts

- The Tree of Life was constructed from an oil rig.
- The Tree of Life is the sixth tallest attraction in Disney World (at 145 feet).
- The Tree of Life is fourteen stories high and 50 feet wide at its trunk.
- 325 animals are carved into the Tree of Life.
- The last animal to be carved into the Tree of Life was a chimpanzee. The artists had actually not included a chimp in the design, but on a visit, it was reported that Jane Goodall asked where the chimpanzee was located. Disney allowed Jane to choose the location for the last carving.

By: hyku

By: Ron and Shannon

Pizzafari

Dining

Animal Kingdom=>Discovery Island

By: hyku

FUN Facts

🎋 The dining area of Pizzafari is divided into six rooms: The Home Room, Nocturnal Room, Upside-Down Room, Camouflage Room, Four Seasons Room, and Bug Room - it is pretty easy to figure out which is which.

Hidden Mickeys

🐾 Find the turtle on the back wall of the dining room just to the left of the ordering station. If you look at the lower left part of his shell, just above his left leg, you can see a goldish three-circle Mickey in a blue background.

By: mrkathika

By: Ron and Shannon

Conservation Station

Animal Kingdom=>Rafiki's Planet Watch

Exhibit

By: mrkathika

Hidden Mickeys

🐭 The huge mural, as you walk into Conservation Station, is simply gorgeous. The lively display of animals has interest all its own - but look closer to see a Hidden Mickey! Look at the yellow butterfly near the tiger's head. On the left wing is a classic three-circle Mickey.

🐭 Look carefully at the mural as you walk into Conservation Station. You can find a great Hidden Mickey in the eye of the ostrich - the classic three-circle Mickey is reflected in his eye.

🐭 Head on the train over to Rafiki's Planet Watch, and proceed into the Conservation Station. Along the front of one of the large viewing windows are a series of glass containers with various specimens - one of the containers is in the shape of a three-circle Mickey head.

🐭 The gorgeous mural, as you enter the building, has many Hidden Mickeys. A rather small one is located on the lizard's left ear - it looks like a small set of three black spots.

ESPN Wide World of Sports Complex   Park

By: John Frost - TheDisneyBlog.com

FUN Facts

🌿 The first race held at the Disney World Race Track was the Indy 200 in January 1996.

🌿 The ESPN Wide World of Sports Complex features an amazing twenty zone audio system - which has 56 HD cameras, and 40 HD video screens - enabling them to broadcast any of the competitions at the complex.

Summit Plummet

Water Ride

Blizzard Beach

By: Ron and Shannon

FUN Facts

❦ The Summit Plummet, a 350 foot water slide at Blizzard Beach, is the tallest, longest, fastest free fall water slide in North America.

❦ Summit Plummet allows guests to free-fall down a thrilling twelve-story water slide.

❦ Until a water park in Brazil built a water slide that was fifteen feet taller and up to five mph faster, Summit Plummet was recognized by the Guiness Book of World records as the tallest and fastest water slide in the world.

❦ Until a water park in Brazil built a water slide that was fifteen feet taller and up to five mph faster, Summit Plummet was recognized by the Guiness Book of World records as the tallest and fastest water slide in the world.

By: Ron and Shannon

By: Ron and Shannon

Teamboat Springs

Blizzard Beach

Water Ride

By: Ron and Shannon

FUN Facts

🦯 Teamboat Springs, a 1,200 foot water slide, is the world's longest group white-water raft ride.

Hidden Mickeys

🐭 As you are disembarking from your wild ride on Teamboat Springs family raft ride, you can't miss this huge Hidden Mickey: located across the exit pool is a classic three-circle Mickey head made out of a family raft and a couple of inner tubes.

🐭 Just before the entrance to Teamboat Springs, look to the right into the snow - you will see a blue Hidden Mickey.

By: Ron and Shannon

By: Ron and Shannon

Typhoon Lagoon   Water Park

By: Ron and Shannon

FUN Facts

☞ Typhoon Lagoon is the most visited water park in the world, with approximately 2.06 million guests in 2008 alone.

Hidden Mickeys

🐭 It is well-known that there aren't many Hidden Mickeys in Typhoon Lagoon. There is one that life guards at this water park can point out - it is in the sidewalk between High and Dry Rental and the bridge that leads to Typhoon Tillie's

🐭 This somewhat obscure Hidden Mickey is found in the Typhoon Lagoon logo that is on much of the merchandise. Look at the shadow formed in the logo, and it is an upside down Mickey head!

🐭 As you are winding your way through the cave, you will come across a locator map near the back of the park. On the map, there is a child wearing a pair of Mickey ears. (You won't find this same Hidden Mickey on other park maps.)

By: Ron and Shannon

By: Ron and Shannon

Blustery Bay

Water Ride

Typhoon Lagoon

By: Ron and Shannon

FUN Facts

🦃 Blustery Bay's waves are among the world's largest artifically created waves.

🦃 Blustery Bay is the size of two football fields.

Hidden Mickeys

🐭 On a clear day, you can see a large three-circle Mickey on the bottom of the Bay.

By: Ron and Shannon

By: Ron and Shannon

Castaway Creek

Water Ride

Typhoon Lagoon

By: Ron and Shannon

FUN Facts

If a guest travels the entire 2,100 foot lazy river, the excursion will take 20-35 minutes (depending on how crowded the park is.)

Hidden Mickeys

The best way to see this Hidden Mickey is from an inner tube in Castaway Creek. As you float under the first bridge near Shark Landing, look at the railing on the right side of the bridge. One of the struts has two small Mickey ears at the bottom.

Crush 'n' Gusher

Water Ride

Typhoon Lagoon

By: Ron and Shannon

FUN Facts

🌱 This innovative water roller coaster includes twists, unique uphill pieces of track, and drops of up to 420 feet!

🌱 Crush & Gusher uses incredibly strong jets that pump 1,350 gallons of water PER MINUTE to shoot guests UP hills on this unique water roller coaster.

Hidden Mickeys

🐭 At the top of Crush 'n' Gusher's elevator, there is a classic three-circle Mickey painted on the concrete to the left.

By: Ron and Shannon   By: Ron and Shannon

Ketchakiddee Creek

Water Ride

Typhoon Lagoon

By: Ron and Shannon

Hidden Mickeys

☺ Look down at Ketchakiddee Creek from Humunga Cowabunga - the three pool areas form a Mickey head.

☺ At the back of Ketchakiddee Creek, look for a hole shaped like classic Mickey. It is in the rock in the back wall of the cave, about a foot and a half from the ground, near the drain at the right side of the cave.

By: Ron and Shannon

By: Ron and Shannon

Shark Reef
Typhoon Lagoon

Water Ride

By: Ron and Shannon

FUN Facts

❦ The leopard and bonnethead sharks found in the Shark Reef are particularly passive.

Hidden Mickeys

🐭 This Hidden Mickey is almost more of a Fun Fact. While reports of Hidden Mickeys in Shark Reef abound, lifeguards at the Shark Reef have regularly replied that the only Hidden Mickeys that exist are created by the lifeguards. So, depending on he day, you may or may not find a Hidden Mickey. Look at the algae on the walls, which are often deliberately formed into Mickeys. Also, look for rocks that are arranged into Mickey heads.

By: Matt Howry

By: Matt Howry

Singapore Sals

Typhoon Lagoon

Shopping

By: Ron and Shannon

FUN Facts

🌴 Singapore Sal's was hit hard by the typhoon. In fact, there are still life preservers and lobster traps on the roof!

Hidden Mickeys

👓 Look on the outside wall of this shop, and you will find a clock, a thermometer, and a barometer that form a classic three-circle Mickey.

By: Ron and Shannon

By: Ron and Shannon

Downtown Disney   Business District

By: Ron and Shannon

FUN Facts

When Downtown Disney opened on March 22, 1975, it was intended to be a shopping districts for the residents of a planned Disney community. When the residences turned into hotel rooms, Downtown Disney evolved into a shopping area for Disney World guests.

Hidden Mickeys

The giant fountain in Downtown Disney creates a Hidden Mickey - but it is best seen from the sky!!

162

Marketplace
Downtown Disney

Region

By: Ron and Shannon

FUN Facts
🦅 The Marketplace section of Downtown Disney has undergone several name changes since its inception, including: Lake Buena Vista Village, Walt Disney World Village, and now, Disney Village Marketplace.

Hidden Mickeys
🐭 You can find a couple of decorative Hidden Mickeys in the overhead Marketplace sign, as you walk into the Marketplace from the bus stop.
🐭 All around the lake, there are subtle Hidden Mickeys in the wrought iron fencing.

By: Ron and Shannon

By: Ron and Shannon

LEGO Imagination Center

Shopping

Downtown Disney=>Marketplace

By: Ron and Shannon

FUN Facts

🖙 Look for the sea serpent in the water near the LEGO Imagination Center - he is made up of over a million Legos, and is around thirty feet long.

🖙 The popular tourist family made out of Lego blocks was updated in the 2011 remodel - now the family includes a father wearing a Goofy hat, a mother wearing mouse ears, a pirate son, and a daughter dressed as Alice in Wonderland.

By: Greencolander

By: sylvar

Once Upon A Toy

Shopping

Downtown Disney=>Marketplace

By: Ron and Shannon

Hidden Mickeys

🐭 Mickey even hides among the toys! Find a classic three-circle Hidden Mickey at the entrance to the Once Upon a Toy store. Look at the top log on each side of the entrance, right next to the words "once" and "upon" - the wheels of the Tonka truck that is balanced on each log create Mickey's ears!

🐭 Be sure to check out the Tinker Toys at the top of the merchandise stands - they form a classic three-circle Mickey.

By: sylvar

By: sylvar

World Of Disney

Downtown Disney=>Marketplace

By: Harshlight

FUN Facts

🪶 The Downtown Disney World of Disney is the largest Disney store in the world, consisting of twelve rooms. At its widest point, the World of Disney is just a little shorter than a football field.

Hidden Mickeys

🐭 Visit the villain's room in World of Disney, to find a unique Hidden Mickey. First, you need to locate the red hand coming out of the wall, holding a wand. Now, take a look at the cuff - nestled among the various spots on the Dalmatian-dotted cuff, you will find that one of the dots is in the shape of a classic three-circle Mickey head.

🐭 "It's Kind of Fun to Do the Impossible" is the expression on a piece of art in the World of Disney, and it also can describe the feeling one gets while discovering Hidden Mickeys! Find the piece of art that looks like a half a compass in a box to find another Hidden Mickey. The compass needle comes right over the blue three-circle Mickey.

Pirates of the Caribbean — Battle for Buccaneer Gold

Ride

Downtown Disney=>West Side=>DisneyQuest

FUN Facts

☝ Look at the booty that is part of the decoration. You will see treasures from other movies, like Aladdin's lamp and magic carpet.

☝ Look for the marooned boat in this Disney Quest attraction; you will find the name Marc Davis on the boat, in honor of the Disney imagineer Marc Davis who designed many of the animatronic figures in Magic Kingdom's Pirates of the Caribbean.

By: Ron and Shannon   By: Ron and Shannon

Cirque du Soleil — La Nouba   Fee-Based Activity
Downtown Disney=>West Side

By: Ron and Shannon

FUN Facts

🌿 La Nouba's 5000th performance was at its 9:00 PM show on July 10th, 2009. Their 6000th performance was at the 6:00 PM show on August 13, 2011.

🌿 To make sure the wigs fit the performers perfectly, plaster head molds were created for the performers that wear hair pieces. Furthermore, four different wig styles were developed for each character, and each of those wig designs took a wig designer around 70 hours to create.

Disney's Boardwalk Inn

Resort-Deluxe

Boardwalk Area

By: Darren Wittko

FUN Facts

☞ Take a close look at the light-up Boardwalk sign - sometimes when you look at it, two letters will seem "burnt out", and at other times, only those two letters are lit. Coincidentally, those two letters are D and W... for Disney World?

Hidden Mickeys

🐭 Visit the charming gardens of the Boardwalk Inn. As you walk through the lovely white archway into the garden, glance up to see the Hidden Mickey that is a park of the white woodwork.

🐭 The carousel in the lobby of the Boardwalk Inn features a white horse with some brown Mickey head spots...

By: Darren Wittko   By: Darren Wittko

Sanaa Restaurant

Animal Kingdom Area=>Disney's Animal Kingdom Villas

By: Ron and Shannon

Hidden Mickeys

🐭 Just after you enter the restaurant, look to the left at the white wall above one of the booths - there is a classic three-circle Mickey centered within what looks like wood paddles.

🐭 You will find classic three-circle Mickeys nestled in the woodwork in the center of many of the solid dining room tables.

Disney's Beach Club Resort

Resort-Deluxe

Yacht And Beach Club Area

By: Darren Wittko

Hidden Mickeys

🐭 As you are walking in the hallway that curves around Cape May Buffet in the Beach Club Resort, be sure to examine the various sand sculpture pieces of art hanging on the walls. In one of the frames, you will find a small plastic Mickey statue, enjoying one of the sand castles.

🐭 As you enter the Beach Club, be sure to take in the sea shell pictures on the left. Three of them form an irregular Hidden Mickey.

By: Darren Wittko   By: Darren Wittko

Beaches & Cream Soda Shop   **Dining**

Yacht And Beach Club Area=>Disney's Beach Club Resort

By: d.k.peterson

FUN Facts

🦌 The Kitchen Sink sundae is immense! It consists of eight scoops of ice cream, every topping offered in the restaurant, including Oreo cookies, candy bars, brownies, bananas, pound cake, and cherries, as well as an entire can of whipping cream.

Hidden Mickeys

🐭 Find the painted design of onion rings high on the wall. Three of the onion rings form a classic three-circle Mickey.

🐭 In the take-out part of Beaches and Cream, look for Minnie - her pearls form a Hidden Mickey near the bottom.

By: Ron and Shannon   By: Ron and Shannon

Yachtsman Steakhouse

Dining

Yacht And Beach Club Area=>Disney's Yacht Club Resort

By: Ron and Shannon

Hidden Mickeys

🐭 When checking in for dinner, peek at the backside of the lantern on the podium. There is a Mickey head peering back at you from the glass.

🐭 On the wall of the Yachtsman Steakhouse, just past the podium, you can find a framed picture of "Mickey Moo", a cow born with a Hidden Mickey on her hide!

By: Darren Wittko

By: Darren Wittko

Stormalong Bay

Point of Interest

Yacht And Beach Club Area

By: Ron and Shannon

FUN Facts

🚩 Stormalong Bay, Disney's Beach Club Resort swimming area, holds 750,000 gallons of water, making it the largest sandy-bottom pool in the world!

🚩 In a 2004 Disney Magazine Reader's Choice poll, Stormalong Bay was chosen as Walt Disney World's best resort pool.

🚩 It has been reported that the original plan was to have fish in Stormalong Bay, but the filtration system caused a problem. The story goes that the million dollar system worked great for fish, but was not able to filter out the sunscreen, which then clogged the fish gills.

By: Ron and Shannon

By: Ron and Shannon

Disney's Wilderness Lodge

Wilderness Lodge Area

Resort-Deluxe

By: mrkathika

FUN Facts

🐾 93% of the visitors at Wilderness Lodge are repeat guests.

🐾 Disney's Wilderness Lodge offers a tour each week, allowing guests to learn interesting inforamtion AND find tons of Hidden Mickeys.

Hidden Mickeys

🐭 Look at the iron braces all throughout the Wilderness Lodge - they are shaped like classic three-circle Mickeys.

By: Darren Wittko

By: mrkathika

Disney's Contemporary Resort   Resort-Deluxe
Contemporary Area

By: mrkathika

FUN Facts
🌱 On November 17, 1973, President Nixon declared that he "was not a crook" at a press conference at the Contemporary Resort.

Hidden Mickeys
🐭 This Hidden Mickey can be seen from the monorail as you are leaving the Contemporary Resort, heading towards the Transportation and Ticket Center. Peek over at the roof of the building out towards Bay Lake (as opposed to the Seven Seas Lagoon), and you can see a full-size Mickey, waving!

By: Betsy Weber   By: Ron and Shannon

California Grill

Dining

Contemporary Area=>Disney's Contemporary Resort

By: Ron and Shannon

FUN Facts

Seventy pounds of vine-ripened tomatoes are served in various dining offerings at California Grill every night.

By: Darren Wittko

By: mrkathika

Disney's Port Orleans Resort-French Quarter

Resort-Moderate

Port Orleans Area

By: Harshlight

FUN Facts

The musical notes across the registration desk at Disney's Port Orleans Resort-French Quarter play out the first verse of "When the Saints Go Marching In."

Hidden Mickeys

You can only see this Hidden Mickey in certain bedrooms. Look for the shelf/coat rack on the wall, and you will find a three-circle Hidden Mickey on the shelf support.

The fabric on the chair seats in some of the rooms in the French Quarter is the backdrop for a classic Hidden Mickey. Look in the pattern for a brown, leafy design, surrounded by a green, leafy design - right in the center you will find the black Mickey head.

The bedspread in some of the rooms at Port Orleans French Quarter has FIVE different Hidden Mickeys throughout the pattern. You will find a green three-circle Mickey at the top center of the pink mask with the blue feather. Then, look in the green and white stripes and you will find a three circle Mickey outline in dark green, surrounded by white flowers. You can also find a larger white Mickey head among the beads. A relatively easy Mickey can be found in the balloon design. Finally, look at the yellow-striped turban to find a three-circle Mickey pendant right in the center.

Riverside Mill Food Court

Dining

Port Orleans Area=>Disney's Port Orleans Resort-Riverside

FUN Facts

The Riverside Mill food court was fashioned to look like a Southern cotton mill. It actually is the home of a cotton press powered by a working 35-foot water wheel.

Hidden Mickeys

Find the Native American statue standing near the bakery, and take a look at his moccasins. There is a black three-circle Hidden Mickey painted on the top of each.

Disney's Wedding Pavilion

Disney's Grand Floridian Resort & Spa

Pavilion

By: Ron and Shannon

FUN Facts

🏴 As part of its 'Weddings of a Lifetime' series, Lifetime TV televised live the very first wedding in Disney's Wedding Pavilion on June 18, 1995.

🏴 The Wedding Pavilion was designed so that the bride could see Cinderella's Castle while she is standing at the altar.

By: Ron and Shannon

By: Ron and Shannon

Victoria & Albert's

Dining

Disney's Grand Floridian Resort & Spa

By: berkielynn

FUN Facts

❦ Disney's only full-time harpist entertains diners at Victoria & Albert's.

❦ Victoria & Albert's makes over 10,000 dessert soufflés a year.

By: berkielynn

Disney's Polynesian Resort   Resort-Deluxe

By: mrkathika

Hidden Mickeys

🐭 Enjoy all the tropical accents in the lobby of the Polynesian - especially the tiki statue with the great light blue Hidden Mickey head on one side. The swirly design of the Mickey head simply is startling, since it doesn't really fit the tropical decor.

By: mrkathika

By: mrkathika

Disney's Coronado Springs Resort

Resort-Moderate

By: mrkathika

FUN Facts

✿ Francisco Vasquez de Coronado, a Spanish explorer in the 16th century, offers his name to Coronado Springs. While he never found the Seven Cities of Cibola where he was searching for rumored gold, explorers in his group did stumble upon the Grand Canyon!

Hidden Mickeys

✿ This Hidden Mickey isn't really concealed, but sometimes it is overlooked. Check out the Coronado Springs sign at the bus stop, and you will see several cut-outs of various Disney characters.

By: mrkathika

By: mrkathika

La Marina Boat and Bike Rental   Marina

Disney's Coronado Springs Resort

By: whiteshark29

FUN Facts

Coronado Springs's marina is located on Lago Dorado, which means "Lake of Gold."

Hidden Mickeys

It might be a little difficult to find, but if you are tenacious, you can locate a classic three circle Hidden Mickey right outside of the Marina. Carved into the concrete of the sidewalk, near the sidewalk, this Hidden Mickey can enhance an outside excursion at Coronado Springs.

Hoop-Dee-Doo Musical Revue

Disney's Fort Wilderness Resort

Dining

By: devilelephant

FUN Facts

🌿 Look for the Lawnmower Tree, located near Pioneer Hall at Fort Wilderness. The tree grew around a classic push mower; not much of the mower is visible, but you can ask a castmember to help you find it.

Hidden Mickeys

🐭 Look for the half circle on the bottom of the deer head at the front of the room hosting the Hoop-Dee-Doo Musical Review. There are two indentations attached to the circle, forming the three-circle Mickey.

By: Serena Skretvedt

By: Serena Skretvedt

Disney's Pop Century Resort   Resort-Value

By: Daryl Mitchell

FUN Facts

🦜 The giant Big Wheel in the Disney's Pop Century Resort would be able to fit a child rider who weighs up to 877 pounds.

🦜 The largest Duncan yo-yos ever created exist at Disney's Pop Century Resort, as the stairwell covers in the 60's section.

Hidden Mickeys

👀 While enjoying a meal in the Pop Century food court, find the short blue wall. Clustered along the wall are several darker blue circles - while not actually joined, the circles loosely form a classic three-circle Mickey head.

By: Darren Wittko   By: Darren Wittko

Disney's All-Star Movies Resort   Resort-Value

By: Darren Wittko

FUN Facts

🎬 If you count the dalmations that you can find all over the All-Star Movies Resort, you will find that there are exactly 101.

Hidden Mickeys

🐭 In the courtyard of the Toy Story area of All-Star Movies is Andy's room - check out the checkers on the checker board and you will find hidden Mickeys on them.

🐭 If you are staying in one of the Mighty Ducks rooms at All-Star Movies, look for Mickeys in the pattern created by the movie projectors on the window curtains.

By: Ron and Shannon

By: Ron and Shannon

Disney's All-Star Music Resort   Resort-Value

By: Ron and Shannon

FUN Facts

🎵 You will find musical notes on the front desk and on the curtains in the rooms of the All-Star Music Resort - the notes are both for "When You Wish Upon a Star."

🎵 It would take about 150,000 beads to fill the maracas located in the Calypso section of the All-Star Music Resort.

🎵 The Juke Box in the Rock Inn section of Disney's All-Star Music Resort can accommodate 4,000 CD; those CDs could play for 135 days without hearing the same song twice.

🎵 The instruments on Jazz Inn at the All-Star Music Resort are longer than one of the busses at Walt Disney World.

🎵 There are 160 albums on the rails of Rock Inn at the All-Star Music Resort.

By: Darren Wittko

By: Darren Wittko

Intermission Food Court

Dining

Disney's All-Star Music Resort

By: Ron and Shannon

FUN Facts

❧ The music notes that are found on the beverage stand at the Intermission Food Court are the music to "Be Our Guest."

By: Ron and Shannon   By: Ron and Shannon

Disney's All-Star Sports Resort   Resort-Value

By: Ron and Shannon

FUN Facts

🐾 It would take more than 20 million 12-ounce cans of Coca-Cola to fill one of the humongous Coke cups at Home Run Hotel in Disney's All-Star Sports Resort.

🐾 It would take nearly 9.5 million tennis balls to fill one of the tennis ball cans at Center Court Hotel in Disney's All-Star Sports Resort.

🐾 While there are many sports figures, equipment, and sporting items throughout the All-Star Sports Resort, you will only find one actual team logo - for The Mighty Ducks.

By: Darren Wittko   By: Darren Wittko

WDW Transportation

Transportation

By: Ron and Shannon

FUN Facts

🌠 The areas of the Magic Kingdom parking lot are named after six of the seven dwarfs - there is no Doc because Imagineers didn't want guests to confuse the boat dock transportation with the Doc section of the parking lot.

🌠 Disney World has the 3rd largest bus fleet in Florida; only Miami and Jacksonville have more busses than Disney.

🌠 Disney World has more than 270 busses.

🌠 Walt Disney World Resort busses drive 20 million miles a year.

🌠 Disney busses drive 10,000 miles a day! (If diesel fuel is $3.80 a gallon, that is $38,000 a day in gas!)

By: Ron and Shannon

By: Ron and Shannon

Monorail
WDW Transportation

Transportation

By: LimeBye

FUN Facts

- The WDW monorails are named for the color of the stripe on the side of each train - red, coral (with a white delta to clearly distinguish it from red), orange, gold, yellow, teal (with white deltas to distinguish it from blue), lime (with white deltas to distinguish it from green), green, blue, silver, black, and peach.

- Since 1971, Disney World's monorails have traveled enough miles to go to the moon and back more than thirty times.

- The monorails at Walt Disney World have a top speed of 55 mph; however they cruise at 40 mph.

- The Monorail was the fastest ride in Disney World until Test Track was Installed in Epcot.

By: Evan_Wohrman

Oak Trail Golf Course
Golf
FUN Facts

- After the Oak Trail Golf Course was completed, Disney offered a total of 99 holes of golf to guests.
- Ron Garl designed the Oak Trail Golf Course. Ron has been awarded "Golf Designer of the Year", and earned a Bachelor of Science degree from the University of Florida, with a specialization in turf grasses.

Osprey Ridge Golf Course ⁣⁣⁣⁣⁣⁣⁣⁣⁣⁣⁣⁣⁣⁣⁣⁣ Golf
FUN Facts

Tom Fazio, the designer of Osprey Ridge, prides himself on never having a project come in late or over budget.

Hidden Mickeys

One of the largest Hidden Mickeys on Disney property, the putting green at the Osprey Ridge is a giant Mickey head!

Our Favorite Resources

By: Ron and Shannon

Index

Printed in Great Britain
by Amazon.co.uk, Ltd.,
Marston Gate.